MASTERING UI UX DESIGN

Theroretical Foundations and Practical Applications

FIRST EDITION

Preface

In the ever-evolving digital landscape, the significance of User Interface (UI) and User Experience (UX) design has never been more paramount. From mobile applications to web platforms, the role of UI/UX design is crucial in creating intuitive, engaging, and efficient user interactions. This book serves as a comprehensive guide to understanding and mastering the intricacies of UI/UX design, providing readers with the knowledge and tools necessary to excel in this dynamic field.

Each chapter delves into a specific aspect of UI/UX design, starting with the foundational principles and moving through advanced techniques and future trends. We begin with an introduction to the basics of UI/UX, exploring its definition, history, and key principles. Understanding user needs is crucial, so we dedicate a chapter to user research methods, persona identification, and user journey mapping.

Design principles are thoroughly examined, highlighting the importance of usability, accessibility, visual hierarchy, and error prevention. The design thinking process is detailed, emphasizing the stages of empathizing, defining, ideating, prototyping, and testing. Information architecture, wireframing, and prototyping are covered extensively to equip readers with the skills to organize and visualize information effectively.

Visual design elements such as color theory, typography, iconography, and animation are explored to enhance the aesthetic appeal of interfaces. Interaction design principles, responsive design techniques, and accessibility considerations are discussed to ensure inclusive and adaptable user experiences.

We also address common UI patterns, UX metrics and analytics, platform-specific design considerations, and advanced techniques like persuasive design and gamification. The book concludes with insights into agile and lean UX methodologies, case studies of successful projects, and a forward-looking perspective on the future of UI/UX design.

This book is designed for aspiring designers, seasoned professionals, and anyone interested in the field of UI/UX. It aims to provide a thorough understanding of the principles, processes, and practices that drive successful UI/UX design. By the end of this journey, readers will be well-equipped to create user-centered designs that are not only functional but also delightful and impactful.

Table of Contents

Chapter 1: Introduction to UI/UX Design

Definition and Importance of UI/UX Design

User Interface (UI) and User Experience (UX) design are critical components in the creation of digital products. UI design focuses on the visual aspects of a product—the look and feel of the interface elements that users interact with. This includes buttons, icons, spacing, typography, color schemes, and responsive design. The primary goal of UI design is to create an aesthetically pleasing interface that is consistent and easy to navigate.

UX design, on the other hand, encompasses the overall experience a user has with a product. It involves understanding user needs, behaviors, and motivations to create meaningful and relevant experiences. UX design considers every aspect of the user's interaction with a product, from the initial discovery to the final interaction and beyond. It is about creating products that are not only usable but also enjoyable and valuable to the user.

The importance of UI/UX design cannot be overstated. Good UI design ensures that users can easily interact with a product, reducing frustration and increasing satisfaction. Effective UX design enhances the overall experience, making it more likely that users will continue to use the product and recommend it to others. Together, UI and UX design play a crucial role in the success of digital products, influencing user retention, engagement, and conversion rates.

In today's competitive market, companies that invest in UI/UX design have a significant advantage. They are able to differentiate themselves by providing superior user experiences that meet and exceed user expectations. This leads to increased user loyalty, higher customer satisfaction, and ultimately, better business outcomes.

As technology continues to advance, the field of UI/UX design is constantly evolving. Designers must stay up-to-date with the latest trends, tools, and best practices to create innovative and effective designs. This requires a deep understanding of both the technical and human aspects of design, as well as a commitment to continuous learning and improvement.

In the following chapters, we will explore the various facets of UI/UX design in greater detail. From understanding user needs to implementing advanced design techniques, this book will provide a comprehensive guide to mastering the art and science of UI/UX design.

History and Evolution of UI/UX

The history of UI/UX design is a fascinating journey that reflects the rapid advancements in technology and changes in user behavior. The origins of UI/UX design can be traced back to the early days of computing, where the primary focus was on functionality rather than user experience.

In the 1960s and 1970s, the first user interfaces were command-line interfaces (CLI), which required users to input text commands to interact with computers. This type of interface was highly technical and not user-friendly, limiting the accessibility of computers to those with specialized knowledge.

The 1980s marked a significant shift with the introduction of graphical user interfaces (GUIs). Pioneered by companies like Apple and Microsoft, GUIs made computers more accessible by allowing users to interact with visual elements such as icons, buttons, and windows. The Macintosh, released in 1984, was one of the first personal computers to feature a GUI, revolutionizing the way people interacted with technology.

As the internet emerged in the 1990s, web design became an essential aspect of UI/UX. Early websites were often text-heavy and difficult to navigate, but as technology advanced, designers began to focus on creating more visually appealing and user-friendly websites. The introduction of Cascading Style Sheets (CSS) and JavaScript enabled designers to create more dynamic and interactive web experiences.

The 2000s saw the rise of mobile devices, leading to the development of mobile UI/UX design. The release of the iPhone in 2007 was a game-changer, introducing touch-based interactions and a new approach to mobile design. Designers had to adapt to smaller screens and new interaction patterns, such as swiping and pinching.

In recent years, the field of UI/UX design has continued to evolve with the advent of new technologies such as virtual reality (VR), augmented reality (AR), and artificial intelligence (AI). These technologies present new challenges and opportunities for designers, requiring them to think beyond traditional interfaces and create immersive and intelligent experiences.

The evolution of UI/UX design has also been influenced by a growing emphasis on user-centered design. This approach prioritizes the needs, behaviors, and experiences of users, ensuring that products are designed with the user in mind. Techniques such as user research, usability testing, and iterative design have become essential practices in the field.

Today, UI/UX design is recognized as a critical discipline in the development of digital products. It encompasses a wide range of skills and practices, from visual design and interaction design to information architecture and user research. As technology continues to advance, the field of UI/UX design will undoubtedly continue to evolve, shaping the future of human-computer interaction.

Key Principles of User Interface Design

User Interface (UI) design is guided by a set of key principles that aim to create interfaces that are visually appealing, intuitive, and easy to use. These principles are essential for ensuring that users can interact with a product effectively and efficiently.

1. **Simplicity**: The interface should be simple and uncluttered, presenting only the necessary information and controls. Users should be able to achieve their goals with minimal effort and confusion. This involves using clear and concise language, straightforward navigation, and intuitive design elements.

2. **Consistency**: Consistency in design helps users learn and predict how the interface will behave. This includes maintaining consistent visual elements such as colors, fonts, and icons, as well as consistent interactions and behaviors. Consistent design creates a sense of familiarity and reduces the cognitive load on users.
3. **Visibility**: Important information and controls should be easily visible and accessible. Users should not have to search for essential elements or guess their location. This principle is about prioritizing the most critical elements and ensuring they stand out in the interface.
4. **Feedback**: Providing feedback to users is crucial for informing them about the results of their actions. Feedback can be visual, auditory, or tactile, and it helps users understand what is happening in the interface. For example, buttons changing color when clicked or loading animations indicating progress are forms of feedback.
5. **Affordance**: Design elements should clearly indicate how they can be used. This concept, known as affordance, ensures that users can easily understand the functionality of different elements. For instance, buttons should look clickable, and sliders should indicate they can be dragged.
6. **Error Prevention**: Preventing errors is more effective than providing error messages. This involves designing the interface in a way that minimizes the chances of user errors. Techniques include disabling irrelevant options, providing clear instructions, and using confirmation dialogs for critical actions.
7. **Flexibility**: The interface should accommodate different user preferences and needs. This includes providing multiple ways to perform actions, supporting both novice and experienced users, and allowing customization where appropriate. Flexible design ensures that the interface can be adapted to various user contexts.
8. **Accessibility**: Designing for accessibility ensures that all users, including those with disabilities, can use the interface effectively. This involves following accessibility guidelines, such as providing alternative text for images, ensuring sufficient color contrast, and supporting keyboard navigation.
9. **User Control**: Users should feel in control of the interface and be able to undo actions if necessary. This principle involves providing clear navigation paths, allowing users to backtrack, and offering undo and redo options.
10. **Aesthetic Design**: A visually pleasing design enhances the user experience. This includes using a harmonious color scheme, balanced layout, and aesthetically pleasing typography. While aesthetics should not compromise functionality, a well-designed interface can create a positive emotional response and improve user satisfaction.

By adhering to these key principles, UI designers can create interfaces that are not only functional but also enjoyable to use. These principles form the foundation of effective UI design and are essential for creating products that meet user needs and expectations.

Key Principles of User Experience Design

User Experience (UX) design focuses on the overall experience a user has with a product. It involves understanding user needs, behaviors, and motivations to create meaningful and relevant experiences. The following key principles are essential for effective UX design:

1. **User-Centered Design**: The user is at the center of the design process. This principle involves understanding the user's needs, behaviors, and pain points through user research and incorporating their feedback throughout the design process. The goal is to create a product that is tailored to the user's needs and provides a satisfying experience.
2. **Empathy**: Empathy is about understanding and sharing the feelings of the user. UX designers must put themselves in the user's shoes to understand their emotions, frustrations, and motivations. This empathetic approach helps designers create solutions that resonate with users on a deeper level.
3. **Usability**: Usability is a key aspect of UX design. It involves ensuring that the product is easy to use and meets the user's expectations. Usability testing and iterative design are essential practices for identifying and addressing usability issues.
4. **Desirability**: Desirability is about creating products that users want to use. This involves designing for aesthetic appeal, emotional engagement, and overall satisfaction. A desirable product not only meets functional needs but also creates a positive emotional connection with the user.
5. **Accessibility**: Accessibility ensures that the product can be used by people with diverse abilities and disabilities. This principle involves following accessibility guidelines and best practices to create inclusive designs. Accessible design benefits all users, not just those with disabilities.
6. **Consistency**: Consistency in design helps users learn and predict how the product will behave. This includes maintaining consistent visual elements, interactions, and behaviors. Consistent design reduces cognitive load and makes the product easier to use.
7. **Feedback**: Providing feedback to users is crucial for informing them about the results of their actions. Feedback can be visual, auditory, or tactile, and it helps users understand what is happening in the interface. For example, buttons changing color when clicked or loading animations indicating progress are forms of feedback.
8. **Efficiency**: Efficiency is about enabling users to achieve their goals with minimal effort. This involves optimizing workflows, reducing the number of steps required to complete tasks, and providing shortcuts for frequent actions. Efficient design enhances productivity and user satisfaction.
9. **Flexibility**: The product should accommodate different user preferences and needs. This includes providing multiple ways to perform actions, supporting both novice and experienced users, and allowing customization where appropriate. Flexible design ensures that the product can be adapted to various user contexts.
10. **Simplicity**: Simplicity is about removing unnecessary complexity and focusing on the essential elements. A simple design is easier to understand and use, reducing the cognitive load on users. This principle involves using clear and concise language, straightforward navigation, and intuitive design elements.

By adhering to these key principles, UX designers can create products that provide meaningful, relevant, and satisfying experiences for users. These principles form the foundation of effective UX design and are essential for creating products that meet user needs and expectations.

The Relationship Between UI and UX

User Interface (UI) and User Experience (UX) design are closely related, yet distinct disciplines. Understanding the relationship between UI and UX is crucial for creating effective digital products. While UI design focuses on the visual aspects of a product, UX design encompasses the overall experience a user has with the product.

UI design is concerned with the look and feel of the interface elements that users interact with. This includes buttons, icons, spacing, typography, color schemes, and responsive design. The primary goal of UI design is to create an aesthetically pleasing interface that is consistent and easy to navigate.

UX design, on the other hand, involves understanding user needs, behaviors, and motivations to create meaningful and relevant experiences. It considers every aspect of the user's interaction with a product, from the initial discovery to the final interaction and beyond. UX design is about creating products that are not only usable but also enjoyable and valuable to the user.

The relationship between UI and UX can be likened to the relationship between the form and function of a product. UI design focuses on the form—the visual and interactive elements—while UX design focuses on the function—the overall experience and usability of the product. Both disciplines are essential for creating successful digital products, and they must work together to achieve a seamless and cohesive user experience.

A well-designed UI can enhance the UX by making the interface more intuitive and enjoyable to use. For example, a visually appealing and easy-to-navigate interface can improve the overall user experience by reducing frustration and increasing satisfaction. Conversely, a poorly designed UI can detract from the UX, even if the underlying functionality is sound.

Similarly, a well-designed UX can enhance the UI by providing a clear understanding of user needs and behaviors. For example, user research and usability testing can inform the design of the interface, ensuring that it meets the needs and expectations of the users. Conversely, a poorly designed UX can lead to an interface that is difficult to use and does not meet user needs, even if it is visually appealing.

In summary, UI and UX design are complementary disciplines that must work together to create effective digital products. While UI design focuses on the visual aspects of the interface, UX design encompasses the overall experience of the user. Both are essential for creating products that are not only functional but also enjoyable and valuable to the user.

Chapter 2: Understanding User Needs

User Research Methods

User research is a critical component of the UX design process. It involves understanding the needs, behaviors, and motivations of users through various research methods. The insights gained from user research inform the design process and ensure that the final product meets the needs and expectations of the users. There are several user research methods that designers can use to gather information about their users.

1. **Interviews**: Conducting interviews with users is a direct way to gather qualitative data about their needs, behaviors, and experiences. Interviews can be structured, semi-structured, or unstructured, depending on the research goals. This method allows designers to explore users' thoughts and feelings in-depth and uncover insights that might not be apparent through other methods.
2. **Surveys and Questionnaires**: Surveys and questionnaires are effective tools for gathering quantitative data from a large number of users. They can be used to collect information about user demographics, preferences, and behaviors. Surveys are particularly useful for identifying trends and patterns in user data.
3. **Observations**: Observing users in their natural environment can provide valuable insights into their behaviors and interactions with a product. This method involves watching users as they perform tasks and noting any difficulties or patterns that emerge. Observations can be conducted in person or remotely, using screen recording tools.
4. **Usability Testing**: Usability testing involves observing users as they interact with a prototype or finished product. This method helps identify usability issues and areas for improvement. Usability tests can be moderated or unmoderated and can be conducted in a lab setting or remotely.
5. **Contextual Inquiry**: Contextual inquiry is a field research method that involves interviewing users in their natural environment while they perform tasks. This method provides insights into the context of use and helps designers understand how users interact with a product in real-world scenarios.
6. **Focus Groups**: Focus groups involve gathering a small group of users to discuss their experiences and opinions about a product. This method allows for group dynamics and the exploration of diverse perspectives. Focus groups can generate rich qualitative data and uncover insights that might not emerge in one-on-one interviews.
7. **Diary Studies**: Diary studies involve asking users to record their experiences and interactions with a product over a period of time. This method provides longitudinal data and helps designers understand how user experiences change over time. Diary studies can be conducted using physical diaries, digital tools, or mobile apps.
8. **Competitive Analysis**: Competitive analysis involves evaluating the strengths and weaknesses of competing products. This method helps designers identify best practices, uncover gaps in the market, and gather insights into user expectations.

Competitive analysis can inform the design process and help position the product effectively.

9. **Card Sorting**: Card sorting is a method used to understand how users categorize and organize information. Users are given a set of cards representing different pieces of content and asked to group them in a way that makes sense to them. This method provides insights into users' mental models and can inform the design of information architecture.

10. **Analytics and Metrics**: Analyzing user data from web analytics, app analytics, and other sources can provide quantitative insights into user behavior. Metrics such as page views, click-through rates, and conversion rates can help designers understand how users interact with a product and identify areas for improvement.

By using a combination of these user research methods, designers can gather comprehensive data about their users and create products that meet their needs and expectations. User research is an ongoing process that continues throughout the design and development lifecycle, ensuring that the product remains user-centered and relevant.

Identifying User Personas

User personas are fictional characters created to represent different user types that might use a product, service, or brand. They are based on user research and real data about users, capturing their goals, behaviors, and pain points. Creating user personas helps designers understand and empathize with their users, ensuring that the design process is user-centered.

1. **Research and Data Collection**: The first step in creating user personas is to gather data about the users through various research methods such as interviews, surveys, observations, and analytics. This data provides insights into user demographics, behaviors, needs, and motivations.

2. **Identifying Patterns and Segments**: Once the data is collected, the next step is to analyze it to identify patterns and segments. Users can be grouped based on common characteristics, behaviors, and needs. These segments form the basis for different personas.

3. **Creating Persona Profiles**: For each segment, a detailed persona profile is created. A persona profile typically includes the following elements:
   - **Name**: Giving the persona a name humanizes them and makes them easier to reference.
   - **Demographics**: Age, gender, occupation, education, and other relevant demographic information.
   - **Background**: A brief biography that provides context about the persona's life and experiences.
   - **Goals and Needs**: The primary goals and needs that the persona has in relation to the product.
   - **Behaviors**: The behaviors and actions that the persona exhibits when using the product.
   - **Pain Points**: The challenges and frustrations that the persona faces.

- ○ **Motivations**: The factors that motivate the persona to use the product and achieve their goals.
- ○ **Preferred Channels**: The communication channels and devices that the persona prefers to use.
4. **Adding Quotes and Scenarios**: To make personas more relatable, adding direct quotes from user interviews and scenarios can be helpful. Quotes provide a glimpse into the user's thoughts and feelings, while scenarios illustrate how the persona would interact with the product in real-life situations.
5. **Visual Design**: Creating visually appealing persona profiles can enhance their effectiveness. Including images, icons, and other design elements can make the personas more engaging and memorable.
6. **Using Personas in Design**: Once the personas are created, they should be used throughout the design process. Personas help designers make informed decisions by keeping the user's needs and behaviors at the forefront. They can be used to guide brainstorming sessions, prioritize features, and evaluate design solutions.
7. **Updating and Refining Personas**: User personas are not static; they should be updated and refined as more data becomes available and as user needs evolve. Regularly revisiting and revising personas ensures that they remain accurate and relevant.
8. **Collaboration and Communication**: Sharing personas with the entire design and development team ensures that everyone has a shared understanding of the users. Personas can be used as a communication tool to align the team's efforts and ensure that the product is designed with the user in mind.

By creating and using user personas, designers can develop a deeper understanding of their users and create products that are tailored to their needs and expectations. Personas provide a human-centered approach to design, helping to ensure that the final product is both usable and enjoyable for the target audience.

User Journey Mapping

User journey mapping is a powerful tool used in UX design to visualize the user's experience with a product or service. It involves creating a visual representation of the user's interactions and touchpoints, highlighting their emotions, pain points, and moments of delight. User journey maps help designers understand the user's perspective and identify opportunities for improvement.

1. **Defining the Scope and Goals**: The first step in creating a user journey map is to define the scope and goals of the mapping exercise. This includes determining the specific user journey to be mapped, such as the process of purchasing a product or onboarding a new user. The goals should outline what the team hopes to achieve, such as identifying pain points or improving the overall user experience.
2. **Identifying User Personas**: User journey mapping is most effective when based on well-defined user personas. Personas provide a clear understanding of the user's needs, behaviors, and motivations, which are essential for creating an accurate journey map.

3. **Mapping the Stages of the Journey**: The user journey is typically divided into stages, each representing a different phase of the user's interaction with the product or service. Common stages include awareness, consideration, purchase, onboarding, and post-purchase. Each stage should be clearly defined and aligned with the user's goals and actions.
4. **Identifying Touchpoints and Channels**: Touchpoints are the specific interactions that the user has with the product or service, such as visiting a website, contacting customer support, or receiving an email. Channels are the platforms or mediums through which these interactions occur, such as desktop, mobile, social media, or in-person. Identifying all relevant touchpoints and channels is crucial for a comprehensive journey map.
5. **Documenting User Actions and Emotions**: For each stage of the journey, document the user's actions, thoughts, and emotions. This includes what the user is doing, thinking, and feeling at each touchpoint. Capturing the user's emotions helps identify moments of frustration, confusion, or satisfaction.
6. **Identifying Pain Points and Opportunities**: Analyzing the user journey helps identify pain points and areas where the user experience can be improved. Pain points are moments where the user encounters difficulties or obstacles. Opportunities are moments where the experience can be enhanced to create delight or improve satisfaction.
7. **Creating the Visual Map**: The visual representation of the user journey can take various forms, such as flowcharts, diagrams, or storyboards. The map should be clear, easy to understand, and visually engaging. Key elements to include are the stages of the journey, touchpoints, user actions, emotions, and pain points.
8. **Collaborating with Stakeholders**: User journey maps are valuable tools for collaboration and communication. Sharing the journey map with stakeholders, including designers, developers, marketers, and customer support teams, ensures that everyone has a shared understanding of the user's experience. Collaborative discussions can lead to actionable insights and improvements.
9. **Using the Map to Drive Design Decisions**: The insights gained from user journey mapping should be used to inform design decisions and prioritize improvements. This may involve redesigning touchpoints, enhancing communication channels, or addressing specific pain points. The goal is to create a seamless and enjoyable user experience.
10. **Iterating and Updating the Map**: User journey maps should be iteratively updated as new data becomes available and as the product or service evolves. Regularly revisiting and refining the map ensures that it remains accurate and relevant, providing ongoing value to the design process.

By creating and using user journey maps, designers can gain a deep understanding of the user's experience and identify opportunities for enhancing the product or service. Journey maps provide a holistic view of the user's interactions, helping to create more user-centered and effective designs.

Conducting User Interviews

User interviews are a fundamental method in UX research for gaining deep insights into users' needs, behaviors, and experiences. Conducting effective user interviews requires careful planning, execution, and analysis. Here are the key steps to conducting successful user interviews:

1. **Defining Objectives**: Before conducting interviews, it is essential to define the objectives. What do you hope to learn from the interviews? Objectives might include understanding user motivations, identifying pain points, or exploring user behaviors.
2. **Recruiting Participants**: Selecting the right participants is crucial for gathering relevant data. Participants should represent the target user personas. Recruitment can be done through various channels such as user databases, social media, and professional networks. Incentives may be offered to encourage participation.
3. **Preparing the Interview Guide**: An interview guide outlines the questions and topics to be covered during the interview. It should include a mix of open-ended questions that encourage detailed responses and follow-up questions to probe deeper into specific areas. The guide should be flexible to allow for natural conversation flow.
4. **Setting Up the Interview Environment**: Conducting interviews in a comfortable and quiet environment helps put participants at ease. Whether in person, over the phone, or via video call, ensure that the environment is free from distractions and conducive to open communication.
5. **Building Rapport**: Establishing rapport with participants is important for gaining their trust and encouraging honest responses. Begin the interview with casual conversation and introduce yourself and the purpose of the interview. Reassure participants that their responses are confidential and that there are no right or wrong answers.
6. **Conducting the Interview**: During the interview, follow the guide but remain flexible. Encourage participants to share their thoughts and experiences in their own words. Use active listening techniques, such as nodding and paraphrasing, to show that you are engaged. Avoid leading questions that may bias the responses.
7. **Probing for Depth**: Use follow-up questions to probe deeper into participants' responses. For example, if a participant mentions a frustration, ask them to elaborate on why it is frustrating and how it impacts their experience. Probing helps uncover underlying motivations and insights.
8. **Recording and Note-Taking**: Recording the interview, with participants' consent, ensures that no details are missed. Additionally, take notes during the interview to capture key points and observations. Transcribing the recording later can aid in detailed analysis.
9. **Analyzing the Data**: After conducting the interviews, analyze the data to identify patterns, themes, and insights. This involves coding the responses, categorizing them into themes, and synthesizing the findings. Tools such as qualitative analysis software can assist in organizing and analyzing the data.
10. **Sharing and Acting on Insights**: Share the insights gained from the interviews with the design and development team. Use the findings to inform design decisions, prioritize features, and address pain points. User interviews provide valuable input for creating user-centered designs.
11. **Iterating the Process**: User interviews should be an ongoing process throughout the design and development lifecycle. Regularly conducting interviews helps keep the

product aligned with user needs and allows for continuous improvement based on user feedback.

By conducting effective user interviews, designers can gain a deep understanding of their users' needs, behaviors, and experiences. The insights gathered from interviews inform the design process and ensure that the final product meets the needs and expectations of the users.

Analyzing User Data

Analyzing user data is a critical step in the UX design process. It involves transforming raw data collected from various research methods into meaningful insights that inform design decisions. Effective data analysis helps designers understand user behaviors, identify patterns, and uncover opportunities for improvement.

1. **Data Collection**: User data can be collected through various methods such as interviews, surveys, observations, usability testing, and analytics. The type of data collected can be qualitative (e.g., user feedback, interview transcripts) or quantitative (e.g., survey results, web analytics).
2. **Data Cleaning and Preparation**: Before analysis, the data needs to be cleaned and prepared. This involves checking for completeness, removing duplicates, and addressing any inconsistencies. For qualitative data, this might include transcribing interviews and organizing notes. For quantitative data, it may involve formatting and structuring the data for analysis.
3. **Coding and Categorizing Qualitative Data**: For qualitative data, the first step in analysis is coding, which involves tagging segments of the data with labels that represent key themes or concepts. This can be done manually or using qualitative analysis software. Once coded, the data can be categorized into broader themes and sub-themes.
4. **Statistical Analysis of Quantitative Data**: Quantitative data can be analyzed using statistical methods to identify patterns, trends, and correlations. Common techniques include descriptive statistics (e.g., mean, median, mode), inferential statistics (e.g., t-tests, ANOVA), and regression analysis. Visualization tools such as charts and graphs can help in interpreting the data.
5. **Identifying Patterns and Themes**: Analyzing the coded qualitative data and the statistical results of quantitative data helps identify patterns and themes. These patterns provide insights into user behaviors, needs, and pain points. For example, recurring themes in user feedback might highlight common frustrations or desired features.
6. **Synthesis and Interpretation**: Synthesis involves combining the findings from different data sources to create a comprehensive understanding of the user experience. Interpretation goes beyond identifying patterns to understanding the underlying reasons behind them. This requires critical thinking and a deep understanding of the user context.
7. **Creating User Insights and Personas**: The insights gained from data analysis can be used to create user personas and journey maps. These tools help visualize the user's experience and guide the design process. Personas represent key user

segments, while journey maps illustrate the user's interactions and touchpoints with the product.

8. **Prioritizing Findings**: Not all insights will be equally important. Prioritizing findings based on their impact on the user experience and business goals helps focus design efforts on the most critical areas. This can be done using techniques such as the MoSCoW method (Must have, Should have, Could have, Won't have).

9. **Communicating Findings**: Sharing the findings with the design and development team is crucial for informed decision-making. This can be done through presentations, reports, or workshops. Visual aids such as charts, graphs, and journey maps can enhance understanding and engagement.

10. **Implementing Insights into Design**: The ultimate goal of data analysis is to inform design decisions. The insights gained should be used to guide the design process from ideation and prototyping to testing and iteration. This ensures that the final product is user-centered and addresses the identified needs and pain points.

11. **Continuous Improvement**: Data analysis is an ongoing process. Regularly collecting and analyzing user data helps keep the product aligned with user needs and allows for continuous improvement. User feedback and analytics should be monitored throughout the product lifecycle to ensure ongoing relevance and effectiveness.

By effectively analyzing user data, designers can gain a deep understanding of their users and create products that meet their needs and expectations. Data-driven design decisions lead to more user-centered and successful products, enhancing both user satisfaction and business outcomes.

Chapter 3: UI/UX Design Principles

Usability and Accessibility

Usability and accessibility are two critical aspects of UI/UX design that ensure a product is both user-friendly and inclusive. Usability focuses on the ease with which users can interact with a product, aiming to create intuitive, efficient, and satisfying experiences. Accessibility, on the other hand, ensures that these experiences are available to all users, including those with disabilities.

One of the primary principles of usability is simplicity. A user interface should be straightforward, avoiding unnecessary complexity. This can be achieved through clear navigation, intuitive controls, and a minimalistic design. Simplified interfaces help users accomplish their goals quickly and with less cognitive load.

Another key aspect of usability is consistency. Consistent design elements, such as buttons, icons, and colors, help users predict the behavior of the interface. This predictability reduces the learning curve and enhances the overall user experience. Consistency should be maintained not only within a single product but also across different products from the same brand.

Feedback is also essential for usability. Users need to know whether their actions have been successful or if an error has occurred. This feedback can be visual, auditory, or tactile. For example, a successful form submission might display a confirmation message, while an error might highlight the problematic fields in red.

Accessibility in UI/UX design involves creating interfaces that are usable by people with a wide range of abilities. This includes those with visual, auditory, motor, and cognitive impairments. To achieve this, designers must consider various accessibility guidelines and standards, such as the Web Content Accessibility Guidelines (WCAG).

One fundamental principle of accessibility is providing alternative text for images. This ensures that users who rely on screen readers can understand the content of the images. Additionally, using high-contrast colors can help users with visual impairments distinguish different elements on the screen.

Keyboard accessibility is another crucial aspect. Many users with motor disabilities rely on keyboards rather than mice. Ensuring that all interactive elements can be accessed and operated via the keyboard is vital. This includes providing clear focus indicators and logical tab order.

Designers should also avoid relying solely on color to convey information. Colorblind users might not be able to differentiate between certain colors. Using text labels or patterns in addition to color can make the information accessible to everyone.

Testing is an integral part of both usability and accessibility. Conducting usability tests with real users can reveal issues that might not be apparent to designers. Similarly, accessibility testing, including automated tools and manual reviews, helps ensure compliance with accessibility standards.

Incorporating user feedback into the design process is essential. Regularly gathering feedback from a diverse group of users can lead to continuous improvements in usability and accessibility. This iterative approach helps create products that meet the needs of all users.

Finally, education and awareness are crucial for promoting usability and accessibility. Designers and developers should be trained on best practices and stay updated on the latest guidelines and tools. Organizations should foster a culture that values and prioritizes usability and accessibility in all stages of product development.

Consistency and Standards

Consistency and standards are foundational elements in UI/UX design, playing a crucial role in creating intuitive and predictable user experiences. When users encounter familiar patterns and behaviors, they can navigate and interact with an interface more efficiently and with greater confidence.

Consistency can be categorized into internal and external types. Internal consistency refers to maintaining uniformity within a single product or system. This includes consistent use of colors, typography, button styles, and interaction patterns. For example, if a blue button represents a primary action on one screen, it should do so on all screens within the product.

External consistency extends beyond a single product to other products from the same brand or even industry standards. Users often bring their expectations from other applications into their interactions with new ones. Adhering to external consistency helps meet these expectations and reduces the learning curve. For instance, familiar icons like the magnifying glass for search or the gear for settings should retain their standard meanings.

Adopting design standards and guidelines is another way to ensure consistency. Platforms such as Apple's Human Interface Guidelines and Google's Material Design provide comprehensive resources on creating cohesive and predictable experiences. These guidelines cover various aspects of design, including layout, navigation, interaction, and visual design.

One of the benefits of consistency is improved usability. When users can predict how an interface will behave, they can complete tasks more quickly and with less effort. This predictability leads to a smoother and more satisfying user experience.

Consistency also contributes to a professional and polished appearance. A cohesive design looks more refined and trustworthy, which can enhance the user's perception of the brand. This is particularly important in competitive markets where users have high expectations for quality and professionalism.

Implementing consistency requires collaboration and communication within the design and development teams. Establishing a design system can be an effective way to maintain consistency. A design system is a collection of reusable components, guidelines, and standards that ensure uniformity across different parts of a product or suite of products.

Documentation is a key component of a design system. It provides detailed information on how to use various components and guidelines, helping designers and developers align their work. Regularly updating the documentation ensures that it remains relevant and useful as the product evolves.

User feedback is invaluable in maintaining and improving consistency. Regular usability testing can identify inconsistencies that might have been overlooked during the design process. Gathering feedback from diverse user groups can reveal different expectations and preferences, guiding adjustments to the design system.

Flexibility within the design system is also important. While consistency is crucial, there should be room for innovation and adaptation. Designers should have the freedom to create unique solutions for specific problems, as long as they align with the overall design principles and standards.

In conclusion, consistency and standards are essential for creating user-friendly and professional interfaces. By adhering to established guidelines and maintaining uniformity, designers can build products that are intuitive, reliable, and enjoyable to use. This not only enhances the user experience but also strengthens the brand's identity and credibility.

Visual Hierarchy and Layout

Visual hierarchy and layout are critical components of UI/UX design that influence how users perceive and interact with information on a screen. Effective visual hierarchy guides users through the content, highlighting important elements and ensuring a smooth and intuitive experience.

Visual hierarchy is the arrangement of elements in a way that signifies their importance. It is achieved through various design techniques such as size, color, contrast, and spacing. Larger elements typically draw more attention, so headlines are often larger than body text. Similarly, using bold or contrasting colors for important buttons can make them stand out.

Another technique for establishing visual hierarchy is the use of alignment and grouping. Aligning related elements creates a sense of order and structure, making the interface easier to scan. Grouping related items together helps users quickly understand their relationship and context. For example, placing a label directly above an input field clearly associates them.

Whitespace, or negative space, is a powerful tool in visual hierarchy. Adequate spacing between elements prevents clutter and improves readability. It allows users to focus on one element at a time, reducing cognitive load. Whitespace also gives the design a clean and modern look.

Layout refers to the arrangement of elements on a screen. A well-structured layout ensures that the content is organized logically and is easy to navigate. Grid systems are commonly used in layout design to provide a consistent structure. Grids divide the screen into columns and rows, helping designers align elements and maintain balance.

One popular layout approach is the F-pattern, which reflects how users typically scan web pages. They start at the top left corner, move horizontally, then vertically down the left side, and repeat this pattern. Designers can leverage this behavior by placing important elements along these paths.

Another effective layout strategy is the Z-pattern, often used in designs with less text and more images. Users scan from the top left to the top right, then diagonally to the bottom left, and finally to the bottom right. Placing key elements at these points can capture attention and guide users through the content.

Responsive design is an essential consideration for layout. With the variety of devices and screen sizes available, a layout must adapt to different contexts. Responsive design involves using flexible grids, images, and media queries to ensure the layout adjusts seamlessly across devices. This provides a consistent user experience, whether on a desktop, tablet, or smartphone.

Consistency in layout across different pages of an application or website enhances usability. Users become familiar with the structure, making it easier to find information and complete tasks. Repeating layout patterns, such as navigation bars and footers, reinforces this familiarity.

Visual hierarchy and layout are closely tied to accessibility. Ensuring that the visual hierarchy is perceivable by all users, including those with visual impairments, is crucial. This can involve using sufficient contrast between text and background, providing text alternatives for images, and ensuring that the layout is navigable by keyboard.

Designers can use tools like wireframes and prototypes to plan and test visual hierarchy and layout. Wireframes provide a basic structure without detailed design elements, focusing on the placement of content. Prototypes offer a more interactive representation, allowing designers to test the flow and functionality before final implementation.

In summary, visual hierarchy and layout are fundamental to creating effective and engaging user interfaces. By carefully arranging elements and guiding users through the content, designers can enhance usability, readability, and overall user satisfaction. These principles are essential for delivering a seamless and intuitive user experience.

Feedback and Response Time

Feedback and response time are critical elements in UI/UX design that significantly impact user satisfaction and overall experience. Effective feedback mechanisms ensure that users are informed about the results of their actions, while optimal response times maintain a seamless interaction flow.

Feedback in user interfaces can be visual, auditory, or tactile. Visual feedback includes changes in button states, progress indicators, and notification messages. For example, when a user clicks a button, it might change color or display a loading spinner, indicating that the action is being processed. This immediate response reassures users that their input has been received.

Auditory feedback involves sounds that confirm actions or alert users to errors. For instance, a beep sound might indicate a successful operation, while an error sound can notify users of an issue that needs attention. Auditory feedback is especially useful for users with visual impairments, providing an additional layer of communication.

Tactile feedback, often used in mobile and wearable devices, includes vibrations or haptic responses. For example, a slight vibration when a button is pressed can confirm the action, enhancing the user's sense of interaction. Tactile feedback is valuable in contexts where visual or auditory feedback might not be as effective.

Response time is the duration between a user's action and the system's response. Fast response times are crucial for maintaining user engagement and satisfaction. Ideally, most interactions should be processed in under a second. When responses take longer, users may become frustrated or confused.

There are several strategies to manage response times effectively. One approach is to provide immediate feedback even if the full action takes longer to complete. For instance, displaying a loading spinner or progress bar can indicate that the system is working on the request. This helps manage user expectations and reduces anxiety about whether the action was registered.

Another strategy is to optimize the performance of the application to minimize delays. This can involve techniques such as caching, asynchronous processing, and efficient coding practices. Ensuring that servers and networks are adequately provisioned can also contribute to faster response times.

Designers should also consider the context of use when evaluating response times. For critical actions, such as submitting a form or completing a transaction, faster response times are essential. In contrast, less critical actions might tolerate slightly longer delays, provided that users are informed about the progress.

Error prevention and recovery are closely related to feedback and response time. Providing real-time validation and feedback can prevent errors before they occur. For example, highlighting an invalid email format immediately allows users to correct it without submitting the form and waiting for a response.

When errors do occur, clear and actionable feedback is crucial. Error messages should be specific, indicating what went wrong and how users can fix it. Providing suggestions or examples can help users understand the issue and take corrective action.

Testing is vital to ensure that feedback mechanisms and response times meet user expectations. Usability testing can reveal whether feedback is clear and timely, while performance testing can identify bottlenecks that affect response times. Iterative testing and refinement help create a more responsive and user-friendly interface.

In summary, feedback and response time are essential for creating engaging and effective user experiences. By providing immediate and clear feedback and optimizing response times, designers can enhance user satisfaction and maintain a seamless interaction flow. These principles are fundamental for building trust and confidence in the user interface.

Error Prevention and Recovery

Error prevention and recovery are crucial aspects of UI/UX design that contribute to a smooth and frustration-free user experience. By anticipating potential errors and providing effective solutions for recovery, designers can enhance usability and user satisfaction.

One of the primary strategies for error prevention is input validation. Real-time validation checks user inputs as they type, providing immediate feedback on errors. For example, if a user enters an invalid email address format, the input field can display an error message and suggest the correct format. This prevents users from submitting incorrect information and reduces the likelihood of errors.

Another effective method for preventing errors is using constraints and affordances. Constraints limit user actions to valid options, reducing the chance of making mistakes. For example, a date picker widget ensures users select a valid date rather than typing it manually. Affordances, on the other hand, provide visual cues about how to interact with elements. For instance, a button with a prominent shadow indicates that it can be pressed.

Providing clear instructions and guidance is also essential for error prevention. Instructions should be concise and placed near the relevant input fields. Tooltips and inline help can offer additional information without overwhelming the user. For example, a password field might include a tooltip with password requirements, helping users create valid passwords on the first try.

Error recovery involves providing users with ways to correct mistakes and continue their tasks. One of the most effective error recovery methods is offering undo and redo options. This allows users to reverse their actions easily, providing a safety net for accidental errors. For example, a text editor might include undo and redo buttons to revert changes made to a document.

Descriptive error messages are crucial for effective error recovery. Error messages should clearly explain what went wrong and how users can fix the issue. Avoid using technical jargon or vague language. Instead, provide actionable steps to resolve the problem. For instance, instead of saying "Error 404," an error message might say, "The page you are looking for cannot be found. Check the URL for typos or return to the homepage."

Contextual help and support can further aid in error recovery. Providing users with access to help documentation, FAQs, or support channels can assist them in resolving issues independently. For example, a help icon near a complex form field can link to detailed instructions or a support article.

Designing for error tolerance is another important consideration. This involves creating systems that can handle user errors gracefully. For example, if a user accidentally closes a tab with unsaved work, the system can prompt them to confirm the action or automatically save their progress. Error tolerance reduces the impact of mistakes and improves the overall user experience.

In complex workflows, offering a step-by-step process with clear navigation can help prevent and recover from errors. Breaking down tasks into smaller, manageable steps with progress indicators allows users to focus on one task at a time. If an error occurs, users can easily identify and correct the specific step rather than redoing the entire process.

Finally, user testing is essential for identifying potential errors and refining prevention and recovery mechanisms. Conduct usability testing with real users to observe how they interact with the interface and where errors occur. Gather feedback on error messages and recovery options to ensure they are effective and user-friendly.

In conclusion, error prevention and recovery are vital for creating intuitive and resilient user interfaces. By anticipating potential errors, providing clear guidance, and offering effective recovery options, designers can enhance usability and reduce user frustration. These principles are key to building reliable and user-centric applications.

Chapter 4: The Design Thinking Process

Empathize: Understanding the User

The first stage of the design thinking process is to empathize with the users, understanding their needs, experiences, and challenges. This stage involves deep user research to gain insights into the user's world and build a foundation for designing solutions that truly address their problems.

Empathy in design thinking means putting oneself in the users' shoes and seeing the world from their perspective. It requires active listening and observation to uncover users' motivations, desires, and pain points. There are several methods to achieve this, including user interviews, surveys, observation, and immersion.

User interviews are one of the most effective ways to gather qualitative data. By conducting one-on-one interviews, designers can ask open-ended questions that allow users to share their experiences and thoughts in detail. It's important to create a comfortable environment where users feel safe to express their opinions honestly.

Observation involves watching users interact with a product or service in their natural environment. This method can reveal insights that users might not be able to articulate. For example, observing how users navigate a website can highlight areas of confusion or frustration that might not be evident from interviews alone.

Immersion takes observation a step further by having designers experience the user's environment firsthand. This might involve using the product as the users would or participating in the users' daily activities. Immersion helps designers gain a deeper understanding of the context in which the product is used and the challenges users face.

Another valuable method for understanding users is creating empathy maps. An empathy map is a visual representation that captures what users say, think, feel, and do. It helps designers synthesize information from various research methods and identify patterns and insights. Empathy maps are typically divided into four quadrants, each representing a different aspect of the user's experience.

Personas are fictional characters based on user research that represent different user types. They help designers keep the users in mind throughout the design process. Each persona includes details such as demographics, goals, needs, and pain points. By referring to personas, designers can ensure that their solutions cater to the diverse needs of their target audience.

Journey mapping is another technique used to empathize with users. A user journey map is a visual representation of the user's experience with a product or service over time. It highlights the user's goals, actions, emotions, and pain points at each stage of their interaction. Journey maps help identify opportunities for improvement and innovation.

It's important to approach the empathize stage with an open mind and without preconceived notions. Designers should be curious and non-judgmental, allowing users to share their experiences freely. This unbiased approach helps uncover genuine insights that might otherwise be overlooked.

Collaboration is also crucial during this stage. Involving team members from different disciplines can provide diverse perspectives and enhance the understanding of users. Workshops and brainstorming sessions can facilitate the sharing of insights and ideas, fostering a collaborative environment.

Once sufficient data has been gathered, it's essential to synthesize and analyze the findings. This involves identifying common themes, patterns, and outliers. Tools such as affinity diagrams can help organize and prioritize insights. The goal is to distill the information into actionable insights that inform the next stages of the design thinking process.

In summary, the empathize stage is about gaining a deep understanding of users and their needs. Through various research methods, designers can uncover valuable insights that guide the design process. By empathizing with users, designers can create solutions that are truly user-centric and address the real problems users face.

Define: Framing the Problem

The second stage of the design thinking process is to define the problem. After gathering insights during the empathize stage, designers synthesize this information to articulate a clear and concise problem statement. This stage is crucial because a well-defined problem sets the direction for ideation and solution development.

Defining the problem involves narrowing down the focus to specific issues identified during user research. It's about making sense of the vast amount of data collected and pinpointing the core problems that need to be addressed. This step ensures that the design efforts are targeted and effective.

A good problem statement is user-centered, focusing on the needs and challenges of the users. It should be clear, concise, and actionable. Instead of framing the problem from a business perspective, it should reflect the user's perspective. For example, instead of saying "We need to increase sales," a user-centered problem statement might be "Users find it difficult to complete their purchases on our platform."

To define the problem, designers often use techniques such as affinity diagrams and "How Might We" (HMW) questions. Affinity diagrams help organize and group related insights, making it easier to identify common themes and issues. By clustering similar findings, designers can see the bigger picture and focus on the most pressing problems.

HMW questions are a way to reframe problems into opportunities. They are open-ended questions that start with "How might we" and encourage creative thinking. For example, if the problem is that users are frustrated with the checkout process, an HMW question might be "How might we simplify the checkout process to make it more user-friendly?"

Once the problem has been defined, it is often summarized in a problem statement or a point-of-view (POV) statement. A POV statement articulates the user's needs, the insights gathered from research, and the challenges to be addressed. It typically follows a format such as: "User [persona] needs a way to [user need] because [insight]."

Creating a clear problem statement helps align the team and stakeholders on the design goals. It serves as a reference point throughout the design process, ensuring that all efforts are directed towards solving the right problem. A well-defined problem also facilitates effective brainstorming and ideation.

In some cases, the problem definition stage might reveal that the initial assumptions were incorrect or that the problem is more complex than initially thought. This iterative process is a natural part of design thinking. It allows designers to refine their understanding and adjust their approach based on new insights.

Collaboration and feedback are essential during this stage. Engaging with stakeholders, team members, and users to validate the problem statement ensures that it accurately reflects the real issues. Workshops and collaborative sessions can help gather diverse perspectives and foster a shared understanding of the problem.

Defining the problem also involves setting criteria for success. These criteria help evaluate potential solutions and measure the effectiveness of the final design. Success criteria should be specific, measurable, and aligned with the user's needs. For example, a success criterion for a redesigned checkout process might be reducing the average checkout time by 50%.

In summary, the define stage is about synthesizing user insights to articulate a clear problem statement. By focusing on the user's needs and challenges, designers can set a solid foundation for ideation and solution development. A well-defined problem guides the design process and ensures that efforts are directed towards creating meaningful and impactful solutions.

Ideate: Generating Ideas

The ideate stage of the design thinking process involves generating a wide range of ideas and potential solutions to address the defined problem. This stage encourages creativity and divergent thinking, allowing designers to explore multiple possibilities before converging on the most promising ones.

Ideation begins with brainstorming sessions, where participants are encouraged to think freely and suggest any ideas that come to mind, no matter how unconventional they may seem. The goal is to generate a large quantity of ideas without immediately judging their feasibility. This free-flowing creativity can lead to innovative and unexpected solutions.

There are various techniques to facilitate ideation. One common method is mind mapping, which involves visually organizing ideas around a central concept. Mind maps help explore different facets of a problem and identify connections between ideas. For example, a mind map for improving a checkout process might include branches for simplifying steps, enhancing security, and improving user feedback.

Another effective technique is sketching, where designers quickly draw their ideas on paper or a whiteboard. Sketching allows for rapid visualization of concepts and helps communicate ideas more effectively than words alone. It also encourages exploration of different design approaches and variations.

Role-playing and scenarios can also inspire creative ideas. By acting out user interactions or imagining how users might experience a product in different contexts, designers can gain new perspectives and insights. For example, role-playing the checkout process from a user's point of view can reveal pain points and opportunities for improvement.

The "Crazy 8s" exercise is a popular ideation technique where participants fold a piece of paper into eight sections and quickly sketch eight different ideas in eight minutes. This rapid-fire approach pushes participants to think beyond their initial ideas and explore a broader range of solutions.

During ideation, it's important to foster an inclusive and non-judgmental environment. All ideas should be welcomed and considered, as even seemingly impractical ideas can spark further creativity or be combined with other ideas to form viable solutions. Encouraging diverse perspectives and collaboration can lead to more innovative outcomes.

Once a wide range of ideas has been generated, the next step is to evaluate and prioritize them. This involves assessing the feasibility, desirability, and viability of each idea. Feasibility considers whether the idea can be technically implemented, desirability examines whether it meets user needs, and viability evaluates its alignment with business goals.

Affinity diagrams can be used to group similar ideas and identify common themes. This helps in organizing and narrowing down the options. Another useful tool is the impact-effort matrix, which plots ideas based on their potential impact and the effort required to implement them. Ideas that offer high impact with low effort are often prioritized.

Prototyping is an essential part of the ideation process. Creating low-fidelity prototypes or mockups allows designers to test and refine their ideas quickly. Prototypes can range from simple paper sketches to interactive digital models. The goal is to validate concepts and gather user feedback early in the process.

User testing during the ideation stage provides valuable insights into how well the ideas address the defined problem. Observing users interacting with prototypes can reveal strengths and weaknesses, guiding further refinement. Iterative testing and feedback loops help ensure that the final solution is user-centered and effective.

In conclusion, the ideate stage is about generating a broad range of ideas and exploring multiple solutions to the defined problem. By fostering creativity, collaboration, and iterative testing, designers can identify the most promising ideas and refine them into viable solutions. This stage is crucial for innovation and creating user-centric designs.

Prototype: Creating Models

The prototype stage of the design thinking process involves creating tangible representations of the ideas generated during the ideation stage. Prototypes allow designers to test and refine their concepts, gather user feedback, and iterate towards a final solution. This stage is crucial for validating ideas and identifying potential issues early in the design process.

Prototypes can vary in fidelity, ranging from simple paper sketches to high-fidelity digital models. Low-fidelity prototypes, such as paper sketches or wireframes, are quick and inexpensive to create. They are useful for testing basic concepts and gathering initial feedback. High-fidelity prototypes, on the other hand, are more detailed and interactive, closely resembling the final product. They are used to test more refined designs and specific interactions.

Creating low-fidelity prototypes is an excellent way to start the prototyping process. These prototypes focus on the layout, structure, and flow of the design without getting bogged down in details. Paper prototypes, for example, allow designers to quickly sketch different screens and simulate interactions by manually manipulating the sketches.

Digital wireframing tools, such as Figma, Sketch, or Adobe XD, enable designers to create low-fidelity digital prototypes. These tools offer pre-built components and templates, making it easy to arrange elements and create interactive prototypes. Low-fidelity prototypes are ideal for exploring different design directions and identifying major usability issues.

Once the basic concept has been validated, designers can move on to creating high-fidelity prototypes. These prototypes include more detailed visuals, interactive elements, and real content. High-fidelity prototypes provide a more accurate representation of the final product, allowing for more thorough testing and feedback.

Interactive prototypes enable users to click through different screens and experience the flow of the design. Tools like InVision, Axure, and Marvel allow designers to create interactive prototypes without writing code. These tools support animations, transitions, and other interactive elements, providing a realistic user experience.

Prototyping is an iterative process. Designers create prototypes, test them with users, gather feedback, and refine the design based on the insights gained. This cycle repeats until the design meets the desired objectives and user needs. Iterative prototyping helps identify and address issues early, reducing the risk of costly changes later in the development process.

User testing is a crucial part of the prototyping stage. Observing users as they interact with prototypes provides valuable insights into usability, functionality, and overall user experience. User testing helps identify pain points, confusing elements, and areas for improvement. It also validates whether the design effectively addresses the defined problem.

During user testing, it's important to create realistic scenarios and tasks that users can perform using the prototype. This helps simulate real-world usage and provides more accurate feedback. Designers should observe users' interactions, ask open-ended questions, and encourage users to think aloud while testing the prototype.

Feedback from user testing should be documented and analyzed to identify common issues and themes. This feedback guides the refinement of the prototype and informs design decisions. Prioritizing and addressing the most critical issues ensures that the final design is user-centered and effective.

In conclusion, the prototype stage is about creating tangible representations of design ideas to test and refine them. By iterating on prototypes and gathering user feedback, designers can validate concepts, identify issues, and move towards a final solution that meets user needs and expectations. Prototyping is essential for creating user-centric designs and minimizing the risk of costly changes later in the development process.

Test: Evaluating Solutions

The test stage of the design thinking process involves evaluating the prototypes with real users to gather feedback, identify issues, and validate the solutions. This stage is crucial for ensuring that the design effectively addresses the user's needs and meets the defined objectives.

User testing is the primary method used in the test stage. It involves observing users as they interact with the prototype and collecting their feedback. The goal is to understand how users experience the design, identify any pain points or confusion, and gather suggestions for improvement.

There are several types of user testing, including usability testing, A/B testing, and remote testing. Usability testing focuses on evaluating the overall user experience, identifying issues, and measuring how easily users can complete tasks. A/B testing compares two or more versions of a design to determine which performs better. Remote testing allows users to test the prototype in their natural environment, providing more contextually relevant feedback.

Usability testing sessions typically involve creating realistic scenarios and tasks for users to perform. These tasks should reflect common use cases and challenges that users might encounter. For example, if testing an e-commerce website, tasks might include searching for a product, adding it to the cart, and completing the checkout process.

During usability testing, it's important to observe users' interactions closely, noting any difficulties or confusion. Designers should ask open-ended questions to understand users' thoughts and feelings as they navigate the prototype. Encouraging users to think aloud can provide valuable insights into their decision-making process and highlight areas for improvement.

Recording usability testing sessions can be beneficial for later analysis. Video recordings allow designers to review the sessions, identify patterns, and share findings with the team. Tools like UserTesting and Lookback offer features for recording and analyzing user testing sessions.

A/B testing involves creating multiple versions of a design and comparing their performance. This method is useful for testing specific design elements, such as button placement, color schemes, or wording. By measuring user engagement, conversion rates, or other relevant metrics, designers can determine which version is more effective.

Remote testing allows users to test the prototype in their natural environment, providing more contextually relevant feedback. Tools like Optimal Workshop and UserZoom enable remote testing by distributing the prototype to users and collecting their feedback online. Remote testing can reach a broader audience and gather diverse insights.

After conducting user testing, the next step is to analyze the feedback and identify common issues and themes. Affinity diagrams and other synthesis techniques can help organize and prioritize the findings. The goal is to identify the most critical issues that need to be addressed in the next iteration of the prototype.

Iterative testing and refinement are essential for creating a successful design. Based on the feedback and analysis, designers make necessary adjustments to the prototype and test again. This cycle continues until the design meets the desired objectives and provides a satisfying user experience.

In conclusion, the test stage is about evaluating prototypes with real users to gather feedback, identify issues, and validate solutions. User testing, including usability testing, A/B testing, and remote testing, provides valuable insights into how users experience the design. Iterative testing and refinement ensure that the final design effectively addresses user needs and meets the defined objectives, resulting in a user-centric and successful solution.

Chapter 5: Information Architecture

Defining Information Architecture

Information architecture (IA) is the practice of organizing and structuring content in a way that makes it easy to understand, find, and use. It involves creating a blueprint of how information is arranged and accessed, ensuring that users can navigate and interact with a website or application efficiently. Effective IA helps users achieve their goals by reducing cognitive load and enhancing usability.

The core components of IA include:

1. **Organization Systems**: These determine how content is grouped and categorized. Common organization schemes include hierarchical, sequential, and matrix structures.
2. **Labeling Systems**: These involve naming conventions and terminologies used to represent information. Effective labeling ensures that users can easily understand and find what they are looking for.
3. **Navigation Systems**: These provide mechanisms for users to move through the information space. This includes menus, links, and other navigational aids.
4. **Search Systems**: These allow users to locate specific information using keywords, filters, and other search functionalities.

The goal of IA is to create a user-centered design that reflects the needs and behaviors of the target audience. It requires understanding user needs, business goals, and the content domain. IA is foundational to the user experience, impacting everything from usability to accessibility.

Principles of Information Architecture

Several principles guide the practice of information architecture:

1. **Clarity**: Information should be presented in a clear and understandable manner. Users should not struggle to interpret labels or navigate the site.
2. **Consistency**: Consistent use of design elements, terminologies, and navigation patterns helps users predict where they will find information.
3. **Flexibility**: IA should accommodate growth and changes over time, ensuring that new content can be integrated seamlessly.
4. **Scalability**: The architecture should support a large volume of information without becoming cluttered or overwhelming.
5. **Findability**: Users should be able to locate information quickly and efficiently, whether through browsing, searching, or filtering.

The Role of User Research in IA

User research is critical in developing effective information architecture. Understanding how users think, behave, and interact with information guides the design process. Common user research methods include:

1. **Surveys and Questionnaires**: These collect quantitative data on user preferences and behaviors.
2. **Interviews**: In-depth conversations with users provide qualitative insights into their needs and experiences.
3. **Card Sorting**: This technique involves users organizing content into categories, revealing their mental models and preferred structures.
4. **Usability Testing**: Observing users as they interact with prototypes helps identify issues and areas for improvement.

Tools for Creating IA

Several tools and techniques aid in the creation of information architecture:

1. **Mind Mapping**: Visual representations of information and its relationships help in brainstorming and organizing content.
2. **Wireframing**: Sketching low-fidelity layouts provides a blueprint of the information structure.
3. **Sitemaps**: These diagrams outline the hierarchical structure of a website, showing the relationships between different pages.
4. **Flowcharts**: These illustrate user paths and interactions, helping to visualize navigation and user journeys.

Challenges in Information Architecture

Designing effective IA comes with challenges:

1. **Content Overload**: Managing large volumes of content without overwhelming users is a significant challenge.
2. **Balancing User and Business Needs**: Aligning user needs with business goals requires careful consideration and compromise.
3. **Evolving Content**: Keeping the IA up-to-date with changing content and user needs demands ongoing attention.
4. **Cross-Platform Consistency**: Ensuring consistent IA across different devices and platforms is crucial for a seamless user experience.

In conclusion, information architecture is a critical aspect of UI/UX design that involves organizing and structuring content to enhance usability and findability. By adhering to key principles and leveraging user research, designers can create effective IA that meets the needs of both users and businesses.

Organizing Information

Organizing information is a fundamental aspect of information architecture. It involves grouping and categorizing content in a logical and intuitive manner. Effective organization helps users navigate a site or application efficiently, reducing cognitive load and enhancing the overall user experience.

Types of Organization Schemes

There are several common organization schemes used in information architecture:

1. **Hierarchical Organization**: This scheme arranges information in a tree-like structure, with broad categories at the top and more specific subcategories beneath them. It is useful for content that naturally falls into distinct categories and subcategories.
2. **Sequential Organization**: This scheme arranges information in a specific order, guiding users through a step-by-step process. It is often used for instructional content or linear workflows.
3. **Matrix Organization**: This scheme arranges information in a grid, allowing users to explore content through multiple dimensions. It is useful for complex content that can be categorized in different ways.
4. **Alphabetical Organization**: This scheme arranges information alphabetically, making it easy to find items by their names. It is useful for content with well-known and consistently named items, such as directories or glossaries.
5. **Topical Organization**: This scheme arranges information by topics or themes, grouping related content together. It is useful for content that covers various subjects and can be logically divided into themes.

Best Practices for Organizing Information

1. **User-Centered Design**: The organization of information should be based on user needs and behaviors. Conducting user research and usability testing helps identify the most intuitive structures.
2. **Consistency**: Maintaining consistent organization patterns across different sections of a site or application helps users predict where to find information.
3. **Flexibility**: The organizational scheme should be flexible enough to accommodate new content and changes over time.
4. **Clear Labeling**: Using clear and descriptive labels for categories and subcategories helps users understand the structure and find information quickly.
5. **Balance**: Avoid over-categorizing or creating too many levels of hierarchy, which can overwhelm users. Aim for a balance between depth and breadth in the organizational structure.

Techniques for Organizing Information

Several techniques can help in organizing information effectively:

1. **Card Sorting**: This user research method involves participants organizing content into categories that make sense to them. It reveals users' mental models and preferred structures.
2. **Affinity Diagrams**: This technique involves grouping related content together to identify patterns and themes. It is useful for organizing large amounts of information.

3. **Mind Mapping**: Creating visual representations of information and its relationships helps in brainstorming and organizing content logically.
4. **Content Audits**: Conducting a content audit involves reviewing existing content to understand its scope, quality, and structure. It helps identify gaps, redundancies, and opportunities for improvement.

Examples of Organized Information

1. **E-commerce Sites**: E-commerce sites often use hierarchical organization, with broad categories like "Clothing," "Electronics," and "Home & Garden," and subcategories beneath them.
2. **Educational Platforms**: Educational platforms may use sequential organization for courses, guiding users through a step-by-step learning process.
3. **Directories**: Directories often use alphabetical organization, making it easy to find entries by their names.
4. **Blogs**: Blogs typically use topical organization, grouping posts by themes such as "Technology," "Health," and "Travel."

Tools for Organizing Information

Several tools can aid in organizing information:

1. **Content Management Systems (CMS)**: CMS platforms like WordPress and Drupal provide tools for organizing and managing content.
2. **Sitemap Generators**: Tools like XML-Sitemaps.com help create sitemaps that outline the structure of a website.
3. **Mind Mapping Software**: Tools like MindMeister and XMind help create visual representations of information and its relationships.

In conclusion, organizing information is a critical component of information architecture. By understanding user needs and applying best practices and techniques, designers can create intuitive and effective structures that enhance the user experience.

Navigation Design

Navigation design is a crucial aspect of information architecture, focusing on how users move through and interact with a website or application. Effective navigation design helps users find information quickly and easily, reducing frustration and improving overall usability.

Principles of Navigation Design

Several principles guide effective navigation design:

1. **Clarity**: Navigation should be clear and understandable, with intuitive labels and logical grouping of menu items.
2. **Consistency**: Consistent navigation patterns across different sections of a site help users predict where to find information.

3. **Simplicity**: Keeping navigation simple and uncluttered reduces cognitive load and makes it easier for users to find what they need.
4. **Feedback**: Providing feedback on user actions, such as highlighting the current page or section, helps users understand their location within the site.
5. **Accessibility**: Ensuring that navigation is accessible to all users, including those with disabilities, is essential for a positive user experience.

Types of Navigation Systems

There are several common types of navigation systems used in web and application design:

1. **Global Navigation**: This provides access to the main sections of a site or application and is typically available on all pages. It often includes a horizontal or vertical menu bar.
2. **Local Navigation**: This provides access to sub-sections within a specific area of the site. It helps users explore related content without leaving the current section.
3. **Contextual Navigation**: This provides links to related content within the body of a page, helping users discover additional information relevant to their interests.
4. **Breadcrumb Navigation**: This shows the user's location within the site hierarchy, allowing them to backtrack to previous levels easily.
5. **Search Navigation**: This allows users to find specific information using keywords and search queries. It is essential for sites with large amounts of content.

Best Practices for Navigation Design

1. **User-Centered Design**: Navigation should be designed with the user's needs and behaviors in mind. Conducting user research and usability testing helps identify the most effective navigation patterns.
2. **Clear Labels**: Using clear and descriptive labels for navigation items helps users understand their options and find information quickly.
3. **Logical Grouping**: Grouping related navigation items together helps users find related content more easily.
4. **Visible and Accessible**: Navigation should be easily visible and accessible from all pages. Hidden or hard-to-find navigation can frustrate users.
5. **Responsive Design**: Ensuring that navigation works well on all devices and screen sizes is crucial for a seamless user experience.

Techniques for Designing Navigation

Several techniques can aid in designing effective navigation:

1. **Wireframing**: Creating wireframes of navigation menus and structures helps visualize and test different designs before implementation.
2. **Card Sorting**: This user research method involves participants organizing content into categories, revealing their preferred navigation structures.
3. **Prototyping**: Developing interactive prototypes allows users to test navigation designs and provide feedback before final implementation.

4. **Usability Testing**: Observing users as they interact with navigation helps identify issues and areas for improvement.

Examples of Effective Navigation

1. **E-commerce Sites**: E-commerce sites often use global navigation with categories like "Men," "Women," "Kids," and "Sale," along with a search bar for quick access to products.
2. **News Sites**: News sites typically use local navigation to organize articles by sections such as "Politics," "Sports," "Entertainment," and "Technology."
3. **Educational Platforms**: Educational platforms may use breadcrumb navigation to show users their location within a course hierarchy.
4. **Corporate Sites**: Corporate sites often use contextual navigation to link to related articles, case studies, and resources within the content.

Tools for Navigation Design

Several tools can aid in designing and testing navigation:

1. **Wireframing Tools**: Tools like Balsamiq and Sketch help create wireframes of navigation menus and structures.
2. **Prototyping Tools**: Tools like InVision and Axure allow designers to develop interactive prototypes for testing navigation designs.
3. **Usability Testing Platforms**: Tools like UserTesting and Lookback help conduct usability testing to gather feedback on navigation designs.

In conclusion, navigation design is a critical aspect of information architecture that impacts the user experience significantly. By adhering to key principles and leveraging user research and best practices, designers can create effective navigation systems that enhance usability and user satisfaction.

Labeling Systems

Labeling systems are an essential component of information architecture, focusing on how information is named and represented. Effective labeling helps users understand and find content quickly, reducing confusion and enhancing usability.

Principles of Effective Labeling

Several principles guide the creation of effective labeling systems:

1. **Clarity**: Labels should be clear and unambiguous, making it easy for users to understand their meaning.
2. **Consistency**: Consistent use of labels across different sections of a site helps users predict where to find information.
3. **Relevance**: Labels should be relevant to the content they represent, helping users quickly identify the information they need.
4. **Brevity**: Labels should be concise, avoiding unnecessary complexity and verbosity.

5. **Usability**: Labels should be easy to read and understand, avoiding jargon and technical terms that users may not be familiar with.

Types of Labeling Systems

There are several common types of labeling systems used in information architecture:

1. **Navigation Labels**: These are used in menus and navigation bars to represent different sections of a site. They help users navigate to the desired content.
2. **Content Labels**: These are used within the body of a page to identify different types of content, such as headings, subheadings, and paragraph labels.
3. **Indexing Labels**: These are used to categorize and tag content, making it easier to search and filter information.
4. **Form Labels**: These are used in forms to identify input fields, helping users understand what information is required.

Best Practices for Labeling Systems

1. **User-Centered Design**: Labels should be designed with the user's needs and behaviors in mind. Conducting user research helps identify the most intuitive and effective labels.
2. **Clear and Descriptive**: Using clear and descriptive labels helps users understand their options and find information quickly.
3. **Consistent Terminology**: Consistent use of terminology across different sections of a site helps users predict where to find information.
4. **Avoid Jargon**: Avoiding jargon and technical terms ensures that labels are easily understood by a broad audience.
5. **Testing and Iteration**: Testing labels with real users and iterating based on feedback helps refine and improve the labeling system.

Techniques for Creating Labels

Several techniques can aid in creating effective labels:

1. **Card Sorting**: This user research method involves participants organizing content into categories and assigning labels, revealing their preferred terminology.
2. **Usability Testing**: Observing users as they interact with labels helps identify issues and areas for improvement.
3. **Content Audits**: Reviewing existing content and labels helps identify inconsistencies and opportunities for improvement.
4. **A/B Testing**: Testing different labels with users and comparing their effectiveness helps identify the best options.

Examples of Effective Labeling

1. **E-commerce Sites**: E-commerce sites often use clear and descriptive labels like "Men," "Women," "Kids," and "Sale" to represent different product categories.

2. **News Sites**: News sites typically use labels like "Politics," "Sports," "Entertainment," and "Technology" to organize articles by topic.
3. **Educational Platforms**: Educational platforms may use labels like "Courses," "Instructors," "Resources," and "Support" to represent different sections of the site.
4. **Corporate Sites**: Corporate sites often use labels like "About Us," "Services," "Case Studies," and "Contact" to organize content and navigation.

Tools for Creating Labels

Several tools can aid in creating and testing labels:

1. **Card Sorting Tools**: Tools like Optimal Workshop and UXtweak help conduct card sorting exercises to gather user input on labels.
2. **Usability Testing Platforms**: Tools like UserTesting and Lookback help conduct usability testing to gather feedback on labels.
3. **Content Management Systems (CMS)**: CMS platforms like WordPress and Drupal provide tools for creating and managing labels.

In conclusion, labeling systems are a critical component of information architecture that impact the user experience significantly. By adhering to key principles and leveraging user research and best practices, designers can create effective labeling systems that enhance usability and user satisfaction.

Search Systems

Search systems are an essential component of information architecture, providing users with the ability to find specific information quickly and efficiently. An effective search system enhances usability, reduces frustration, and improves the overall user experience.

Principles of Effective Search Systems

Several principles guide the creation of effective search systems:

1. **Relevance**: Search results should be relevant to the user's query, providing the most accurate and useful information.
2. **Speed**: Search systems should deliver results quickly, minimizing wait times and keeping users engaged.
3. **Usability**: The search interface should be easy to use, with clear input fields, intuitive controls, and helpful feedback.
4. **Flexibility**: Search systems should accommodate different types of queries, including keywords, phrases, and natural language.
5. **Accuracy**: Search results should be accurate and free from errors, helping users find the information they need.

Components of Search Systems

There are several key components of search systems:

1. **Search Interface**: This includes the input field, search button, and any additional controls or filters. The interface should be clear and intuitive, guiding users to perform searches easily.
2. **Search Algorithm**: This is the underlying technology that processes queries and retrieves results. Effective algorithms prioritize relevance, accuracy, and speed.
3. **Search Results**: This includes the list of results returned by the search system. Results should be clearly presented, with relevant information and links to the content.
4. **Filters and Facets**: These allow users to refine and narrow down search results based on specific criteria, such as categories, dates, and tags.

Best Practices for Search Systems

1. **Clear Input Fields**: Search input fields should be clearly labeled and easy to find, encouraging users to perform searches.
2. **Autocomplete and Suggestions**: Providing autocomplete and search suggestions helps users formulate queries and discover relevant content more easily.
3. **Relevance Ranking**: Prioritizing the most relevant results ensures that users find the information they need quickly.
4. **Error Handling**: Providing helpful error messages and suggestions for misspelled or ambiguous queries improves the search experience.
5. **Responsive Design**: Ensuring that the search system works well on all devices and screen sizes is crucial for a seamless user experience.

Techniques for Designing Search Systems

Several techniques can aid in designing effective search systems:

1. **User Research**: Conducting user research helps identify common search behaviors, needs, and pain points, informing the design of the search system.
2. **Usability Testing**: Observing users as they interact with the search system helps identify issues and areas for improvement.
3. **A/B Testing**: Testing different search interfaces and algorithms with users and comparing their effectiveness helps identify the best options.
4. **Analytics**: Analyzing search data, such as common queries and click-through rates, helps identify trends and areas for improvement.

Examples of Effective Search Systems

1. **E-commerce Sites**: E-commerce sites often use search systems with filters and facets to help users find products based on categories, prices, brands, and other criteria.
2. **News Sites**: News sites typically provide search systems that allow users to find articles based on keywords, topics, and dates.
3. **Educational Platforms**: Educational platforms may use search systems that allow users to find courses, instructors, and resources based on specific criteria.
4. **Corporate Sites**: Corporate sites often use search systems to help users find information about services, case studies, and contact details.

Tools for Designing Search Systems

Several tools can aid in designing and testing search systems:

1. **Prototyping Tools**: Tools like InVision and Axure allow designers to develop interactive prototypes for testing search interfaces.
2. **Usability Testing Platforms**: Tools like UserTesting and Lookback help conduct usability testing to gather feedback on search systems.
3. **Analytics Tools**: Tools like Google Analytics and Hotjar help analyze search data and identify trends and areas for improvement.

In conclusion, search systems are a critical component of information architecture that impact the user experience significantly. By adhering to key principles and leveraging user research and best practices, designers can create effective search systems that enhance usability and user satisfaction.

Chapter 6: Wireframing and Prototyping

Basics of Wireframing

Wireframing is a crucial step in the UI/UX design process, providing a visual blueprint of a website or application's layout and structure. It focuses on the placement of elements such as navigation, content, and interactive features, without delving into detailed design elements like color schemes and typography.

Importance of Wireframing

Wireframes serve several important purposes:

1. **Visualization**: Wireframes help visualize the basic structure of a page or screen, providing a clear understanding of how content and functionality will be arranged.
2. **Communication**: Wireframes facilitate communication among stakeholders, including designers, developers, and clients, ensuring everyone has a shared understanding of the layout and functionality.
3. **Iteration**: Wireframes allow for quick iterations and modifications, making it easier to test different layouts and identify the most effective solutions.
4. **Focus on Functionality**: By stripping away design elements, wireframes emphasize the core functionality and user experience, ensuring that the layout meets user needs before moving on to detailed design.

Types of Wireframes

There are several types of wireframes, each serving different purposes:

1. **Low-Fidelity Wireframes**: These are basic sketches or outlines that focus on the overall layout and structure. They are quick to create and ideal for early-stage brainstorming and iteration.
2. **High-Fidelity Wireframes**: These are more detailed and include specific elements like text, buttons, and images. They provide a clearer picture of the final product and are useful for more advanced stages of design.
3. **Annotated Wireframes**: These include notes and annotations explaining the functionality and behavior of different elements. They are useful for communicating detailed requirements to developers.

Best Practices for Wireframing

1. **Start Simple**: Begin with low-fidelity wireframes to explore different layout options and iterate quickly.
2. **Focus on User Needs**: Design wireframes with the user's needs and goals in mind, ensuring that the layout supports an intuitive and efficient user experience.
3. **Use Consistent Elements**: Maintain consistency in the placement and design of elements across different wireframes to create a cohesive user experience.

4. **Involve Stakeholders**: Share wireframes with stakeholders early and often to gather feedback and ensure alignment with project goals.
5. **Keep It Flexible**: Be prepared to iterate and make changes based on feedback and testing results.

Tools for Wireframing

Several tools can aid in the wireframing process:

1. **Sketch**: A popular design tool with robust wireframing capabilities, allowing for the creation of both low-fidelity and high-fidelity wireframes.
2. **Adobe XD**: A versatile design tool that supports wireframing, prototyping, and collaboration.
3. **Balsamiq**: A tool specifically designed for low-fidelity wireframing, with a simple and intuitive interface.
4. **Figma**: A cloud-based design tool that supports real-time collaboration and wireframing.

Example Wireframe Elements

1. **Navigation Bars**: Indicate the placement and structure of navigation menus, including primary and secondary links.
2. **Content Blocks**: Outline the placement of text, images, and other content elements.
3. **Interactive Elements**: Include placeholders for buttons, forms, and other interactive features.
4. **Headers and Footers**: Define the layout and content of headers and footers, including logos, navigation links, and contact information.

Challenges in Wireframing

Wireframing comes with several challenges:

1. **Balancing Detail and Flexibility**: Striking the right balance between providing enough detail to be useful and keeping wireframes flexible for iteration can be challenging.
2. **Stakeholder Buy-In**: Getting stakeholders to understand and appreciate the value of wireframes, especially low-fidelity ones, can be difficult.
3. **Transition to High-Fidelity Design**: Ensuring a smooth transition from wireframes to high-fidelity designs requires careful planning and communication.

In conclusion, wireframing is a vital step in the UI/UX design process, providing a visual blueprint of the layout and structure of a website or application. By focusing on functionality and user needs, wireframes help create a solid foundation for detailed design and development.

Tools for Wireframing

Wireframing is an essential step in the design process, and using the right tools can significantly enhance efficiency and collaboration. Various tools are available, each with unique features tailored to different aspects of wireframing.

Popular Wireframing Tools

1. **Sketch**: A widely-used design tool known for its robust wireframing capabilities. Sketch allows designers to create both low-fidelity and high-fidelity wireframes, with a vast library of plugins and integrations to enhance functionality.
2. **Adobe XD**: Adobe XD offers a comprehensive solution for wireframing, prototyping, and collaboration. Its intuitive interface and integration with other Adobe products make it a popular choice for designers.
3. **Balsamiq**: Balsamiq is designed specifically for low-fidelity wireframing. Its simple and user-friendly interface makes it easy to create basic wireframes quickly, ideal for early-stage brainstorming and iteration.
4. **Figma**: A cloud-based design tool that supports real-time collaboration, Figma is excellent for teams working remotely. It offers robust wireframing features, including components and reusable styles.
5. **Axure RP**: Axure RP is a powerful tool for creating detailed wireframes and interactive prototypes. It is particularly useful for complex projects that require advanced functionality and documentation.
6. **InVision**: InVision is a popular tool for creating interactive wireframes and prototypes. It also offers collaboration features, allowing teams to share and gather feedback on designs easily.

Features to Look for in Wireframing Tools

When choosing a wireframing tool, consider the following features:

1. **Ease of Use**: The tool should have an intuitive interface that allows designers to create wireframes quickly and efficiently.
2. **Collaboration**: Look for tools that support real-time collaboration and feedback, essential for team-based projects.
3. **Integration**: Integration with other design and development tools can streamline the workflow and enhance productivity.
4. **Flexibility**: The tool should support both low-fidelity and high-fidelity wireframing, allowing for different levels of detail as the project progresses.
5. **Prototyping**: Built-in prototyping features can help visualize and test interactions early in the design process.

Best Practices for Using Wireframing Tools

1. **Start with Low-Fidelity**: Begin with low-fidelity wireframes to explore different layout options and iterate quickly. This approach allows for rapid experimentation and feedback.
2. **Leverage Templates and Components**: Use templates and reusable components to maintain consistency and save time. Many wireframing tools offer libraries of pre-built elements.

3. **Collaborate Early and Often**: Involve stakeholders and team members in the wireframing process from the start. Real-time collaboration features can facilitate communication and ensure alignment.
4. **Keep It Simple**: Focus on the structure and functionality of the wireframe rather than detailed design elements. This helps keep the wireframe clear and easy to understand.
5. **Iterate Based on Feedback**: Gather feedback from users and stakeholders and iterate on the wireframe accordingly. Continuous improvement is key to creating effective designs.

Examples of Effective Wireframing

1. **E-commerce Sites**: Wireframing tools can be used to create detailed layouts of product pages, checkout processes, and user account sections.
2. **Mobile Apps**: Wireframing tools help design the structure and flow of mobile app screens, ensuring a seamless user experience across different devices.
3. **Corporate Websites**: Wireframing tools are useful for designing the layout of corporate websites, including navigation menus, content sections, and contact forms.
4. **Educational Platforms**: Wireframing tools aid in designing the structure of online courses, including navigation, content delivery, and interactive elements.

Challenges in Using Wireframing Tools

1. **Learning Curve**: Some wireframing tools have a steep learning curve, requiring time and effort to master.
2. **Tool Overload**: With so many tools available, choosing the right one for a specific project can be overwhelming.
3. **Integration Issues**: Ensuring seamless integration with other tools in the design and development workflow can be challenging.

In conclusion, wireframing tools are essential for creating effective and efficient wireframes. By choosing the right tool and following best practices, designers can enhance collaboration, streamline the design process, and create intuitive and user-friendly layouts.

Creating Low-Fidelity Prototypes

Low-fidelity prototypes are an essential part of the design process, providing a simple and cost-effective way to test ideas and gather feedback early in the project. These prototypes focus on functionality and user flow rather than detailed design, making them ideal for quick iteration and validation.

Importance of Low-Fidelity Prototypes

1. **Quick Iteration**: Low-fidelity prototypes can be created and modified quickly, allowing for rapid experimentation and iteration.
2. **Cost-Effective**: These prototypes are inexpensive to produce, making them ideal for exploring multiple ideas without significant investment.

3. **Focus on Functionality**: By stripping away design details, low-fidelity prototypes emphasize the core functionality and user experience, helping identify potential issues early.
4. **Early Feedback**: Low-fidelity prototypes can be shared with stakeholders and users early in the process, providing valuable feedback and insights.

Creating Low-Fidelity Prototypes

1. **Sketching**: Start with simple sketches on paper or whiteboards to explore different layout and interaction ideas. Sketching is quick and flexible, allowing for rapid changes.
2. **Wireframing Tools**: Use wireframing tools like Balsamiq, Sketch, or Adobe XD to create digital low-fidelity prototypes. These tools offer libraries of pre-built elements and templates to speed up the process.
3. **Clickable Prototypes**: Create clickable prototypes that simulate basic interactions and navigation. Tools like InVision and Figma allow you to link wireframes and create simple interactive flows.
4. **Annotated Prototypes**: Add annotations and notes to explain the functionality and behavior of different elements. This helps communicate the prototype's purpose and gather focused feedback.

Best Practices for Low-Fidelity Prototypes

1. **Keep It Simple**: Focus on the essential elements and interactions, avoiding detailed design and visual elements.
2. **Test Early and Often**: Share prototypes with users and stakeholders early and gather feedback. Use this feedback to iterate and improve the design.
3. **Use Realistic Scenarios**: Create scenarios and tasks that reflect real user needs and behaviors. This helps ensure that the prototype addresses actual user problems.
4. **Be Open to Change**: Low-fidelity prototypes are meant to be flexible and adaptable. Be prepared to make changes based on feedback and testing results.

Examples of Low-Fidelity Prototypes

1. **E-commerce Checkout Flow**: A low-fidelity prototype of an e-commerce checkout flow might include basic wireframes of the cart, shipping, and payment pages, with clickable links to simulate navigation.
2. **Mobile App Onboarding**: A low-fidelity prototype of a mobile app's onboarding process might include wireframes of the welcome screen, tutorial steps, and account creation form, with simple interactions.
3. **Corporate Website Navigation**: A low-fidelity prototype of a corporate website's navigation might include wireframes of the main menu, submenus, and key pages, with clickable links to test the flow.

Tools for Creating Low-Fidelity Prototypes

Several tools can aid in creating low-fidelity prototypes:

1. **Balsamiq**: Known for its low-fidelity wireframing capabilities, Balsamiq offers a simple and intuitive interface for creating basic prototypes.
2. **Sketch**: Sketch provides robust wireframing and prototyping features, allowing designers to create clickable low-fidelity prototypes.
3. **Adobe XD**: Adobe XD offers wireframing, prototyping, and collaboration features, making it a versatile tool for low-fidelity prototypes.
4. **InVision**: InVision allows designers to create clickable prototypes from wireframes, with features for feedback and collaboration.

Challenges in Creating Low-Fidelity Prototypes

1. **Balancing Simplicity and Detail**: Striking the right balance between simplicity and providing enough detail to convey the functionality can be challenging.
2. **Communicating Intent**: Ensuring that stakeholders and users understand the purpose and limitations of low-fidelity prototypes requires clear communication.
3. **Gathering Meaningful Feedback**: Collecting actionable feedback from low-fidelity prototypes can be difficult, as users may focus on missing details rather than functionality.

In conclusion, low-fidelity prototypes are a valuable tool in the design process, providing a cost-effective and flexible way to test ideas and gather feedback. By focusing on functionality and user flow, designers can identify potential issues early and iterate quickly to create effective and user-friendly designs.

Developing High-Fidelity Prototypes

High-fidelity prototypes are detailed, interactive representations of a product, closely resembling the final design. These prototypes include detailed design elements, such as color schemes, typography, and images, providing a more realistic experience for users and stakeholders.

Importance of High-Fidelity Prototypes

1. **Realistic User Testing**: High-fidelity prototypes allow for realistic user testing providing insights into how users will interact with the final product.
2. **Detailed Feedback**: These prototypes enable stakeholders and users to provide detailed feedback on design elements, interactions, and overall user experience.
3. **Stakeholder Buy-In**: High-fidelity prototypes help communicate the design vision to stakeholders, facilitating approval and buy-in.
4. **Development Blueprint**: They serve as a detailed blueprint for developers, reducing ambiguity and ensuring the final product aligns with the design.

Creating High-Fidelity Prototypes

1. **Design Tools**: Use design tools like Sketch, Adobe XD, or Figma to create detailed mockups of each screen, incorporating design elements like colors, fonts, and images.

2. **Interactive Prototyping Tools**: Tools like InVision, Axure, and Adobe XD allow designers to add interactivity to high-fidelity prototypes, creating realistic user flows and interactions.
3. **Design Systems**: Utilize design systems and component libraries to maintain consistency and speed up the prototyping process.
4. **Collaboration**: Involve stakeholders and team members in the prototyping process, gathering feedback and making adjustments as needed.

Best Practices for High-Fidelity Prototypes

1. **Maintain Consistency**: Ensure consistency in design elements, such as colors, fonts, and spacing, across all screens and interactions.
2. **Focus on User Experience**: Prioritize user experience by designing intuitive and efficient interactions and flows.
3. **Test Interactions**: Conduct thorough testing of interactions and user flows to identify and address any usability issues.
4. **Gather Detailed Feedback**: Use high-fidelity prototypes to gather detailed feedback from users and stakeholders, refining the design based on their input.

Examples of High-Fidelity Prototypes

1. **E-commerce Product Page**: A high-fidelity prototype of an e-commerce product page might include detailed images, product descriptions, pricing, and interactive elements like add-to-cart buttons and reviews.
2. **Mobile App Dashboard**: A high-fidelity prototype of a mobile app dashboard might include detailed charts, icons, and interactive widgets, providing a realistic experience for users.
3. **Corporate Website Home Page**: A high-fidelity prototype of a corporate website's home page might include detailed images, typography, and interactive elements like sliders and call-to-action buttons.

Tools for Creating High-Fidelity Prototypes

Several tools can aid in creating high-fidelity prototypes:

1. **Sketch**: A popular design tool for creating detailed mockups and interactive prototypes.
2. **Adobe XD**: A versatile tool for designing, prototyping, and collaborating on high-fidelity prototypes.
3. **Figma**: A cloud-based design tool that supports real-time collaboration and high-fidelity prototyping.
4. **InVision**: A tool for creating interactive high-fidelity prototypes, with features for feedback and collaboration.

Challenges in Creating High-Fidelity Prototypes

1. **Time and Effort**: Creating high-fidelity prototypes requires significant time and effort, making it essential to prioritize the most critical screens and interactions.

2. **Balancing Detail and Flexibility**: Striking the right balance between providing detailed design and maintaining flexibility for iteration can be challenging.
3. **Managing Feedback**: Gathering and managing detailed feedback from users and stakeholders can be time-consuming and complex.

In conclusion, high-fidelity prototypes are a valuable tool in the design process, providing a realistic representation of the final product and enabling detailed testing and feedback. By focusing on user experience and maintaining consistency, designers can create effective and user-friendly high-fidelity prototypes.

Usability Testing of Prototypes

Usability testing is a crucial step in the design process, involving the evaluation of a prototype with real users to identify issues and gather feedback. It helps ensure that the design meets user needs and provides a positive user experience.

Importance of Usability Testing

1. **Identify Issues Early**: Usability testing helps identify design and functionality issues early in the process, reducing the cost and effort of making changes later.
2. **Gather User Feedback**: It provides valuable insights into how users interact with the prototype, highlighting areas for improvement.
3. **Validate Design Decisions**: Usability testing validates design decisions by confirming that the prototype meets user needs and expectations.
4. **Enhance User Experience**: By addressing usability issues, designers can create a more intuitive and user-friendly product.

Conducting Usability Testing

1. **Define Objectives**: Clearly define the objectives of the usability test, such as specific tasks or interactions you want to evaluate.
2. **Recruit Participants**: Recruit participants who represent the target audience, ensuring a diverse and representative sample.
3. **Create Test Scenarios**: Develop realistic scenarios and tasks for participants to complete, reflecting common user goals and behaviors.
4. **Conduct the Test**: Observe participants as they interact with the prototype, taking notes on their behavior, comments, and any issues they encounter.
5. **Analyze Results**: Analyze the results of the usability test, identifying patterns, issues, and areas for improvement.
6. **Iterate and Improve**: Use the insights gathered from usability testing to iterate and improve the prototype, addressing any identified issues.

Best Practices for Usability Testing

1. **Test Early and Often**: Conduct usability testing early in the design process and continue testing at different stages to ensure continuous improvement.

2. **Create Realistic Tasks**: Develop tasks that reflect actual user goals and behaviors, providing meaningful insights into the prototype's usability.
3. **Encourage Think-Aloud Protocol**: Ask participants to think aloud as they interact with the prototype, providing insights into their thought processes and decision-making.
4. **Avoid Leading Questions**: Ask open-ended questions and avoid leading participants, ensuring unbiased and genuine feedback.
5. **Focus on Critical Tasks**: Prioritize testing of critical tasks and interactions that are essential to the user experience.

Examples of Usability Testing

1. **E-commerce Checkout Flow**: Usability testing of an e-commerce checkout flow might involve tasks such as adding items to the cart, entering shipping information, and completing the purchase.
2. **Mobile App Onboarding**: Usability testing of a mobile app's onboarding process might involve tasks such as signing up, completing the tutorial, and exploring key features.
3. **Corporate Website Navigation**: Usability testing of a corporate website's navigation might involve tasks such as finding specific information, contacting support, and exploring different sections of the site.

Tools for Usability Testing

Several tools can aid in conducting usability testing:

1. **UserTesting**: A platform for conducting remote usability tests, with features for recording sessions and gathering feedback.
2. **Lookback**: A tool for conducting live and recorded usability tests, with features for annotating and analyzing sessions.
3. **Optimal Workshop**: A suite of usability testing tools, including card sorting, tree testing, and first-click testing.
4. **Hotjar**: A tool for gathering user feedback through surveys, heatmaps, and session recordings.

Challenges in Usability Testing

1. **Recruiting Participants**: Finding and recruiting representative participants can be time-consuming and challenging.
2. **Managing Logistics**: Coordinating the logistics of usability testing, such as scheduling sessions and managing equipment, can be complex.
3. **Analyzing Data**: Analyzing the data collected from usability tests and identifying actionable insights requires careful consideration and expertise.

In conclusion, usability testing is a vital part of the design process, providing valuable insights into how users interact with a prototype and highlighting areas for improvement. By conducting thorough usability testing and iterating based on feedback, designers can create user-friendly and effective products that meet user needs and expectations.

Chapter 7: Visual Design Elements

Color Theory and Psychology

Color theory is the study of how colors interact with each other and the effects they have on viewers. It's a crucial aspect of visual design because colors can evoke emotions, convey messages, and affect user behavior.

Understanding the color wheel is the first step in mastering color theory. The color wheel consists of primary colors (red, blue, yellow), secondary colors (green, orange, purple), and tertiary colors (a mix of primary and secondary colors). These colors can be arranged to show relationships such as complementary (opposite on the wheel), analogous (adjacent on the wheel), and triadic (three colors evenly spaced around the wheel).

Psychology of color involves understanding how different colors impact human emotions and behaviors. For instance, red can evoke feelings of excitement or urgency, making it effective for call-to-action buttons. Blue is often associated with trust and calmness, making it popular for corporate websites.

Choosing a color scheme involves selecting a base color and then using various color theory techniques to create a harmonious palette. Monochromatic schemes use variations in lightness and saturation of a single color. Analogous schemes use colors next to each other on the color wheel, creating a harmonious and serene look. Complementary schemes use colors opposite each other on the wheel, providing a high-contrast and vibrant look.

Designers should also consider cultural differences in color meanings. For example, while white is often associated with purity in Western cultures, it can signify mourning in some Eastern cultures. It's important to research and understand the target audience when choosing colors.

Color accessibility is another important factor. Designers must ensure sufficient contrast between text and background colors to make content readable for people with visual impairments. Tools like contrast checkers can help evaluate color combinations for accessibility compliance.

Using color consistently helps create a cohesive user experience. Establishing a color system for primary actions, secondary actions, and background elements ensures that users can easily navigate and interact with the interface.

A/B testing different color schemes can provide insights into user preferences and behaviors. For example, testing different button colors can reveal which color drives higher engagement or conversion rates.

Gradients and color transitions can add depth and dimension to a design. Subtle gradients can create a modern and polished look, while bold gradients can make elements stand out.

Incorporating brand colors consistently across all touchpoints strengthens brand identity. A strong brand color palette helps users instantly recognize and associate the design with the brand.

Color theory and psychology are integral to creating visually appealing and effective designs. By understanding how colors interact and the emotions they evoke, designers can create interfaces that not only look good but also enhance the user experience.

Typography and Readability

Typography is the art and technique of arranging type to make written language legible, readable, and visually appealing. It involves choosing fonts, adjusting spacing, and arranging text on the page.

Font selection is a critical aspect of typography. Different fonts convey different tones and personalities. For instance, serif fonts like Times New Roman convey a classic and traditional feel, while sans-serif fonts like Helvetica offer a modern and clean look.

Readability refers to how easily text can be read and understood. It involves factors such as font size, line height, and letter spacing. Optimal readability is achieved when these elements are balanced to reduce eye strain and make text easily scannable.

Line length is another important factor in readability. Text that is too wide can be difficult to follow from one line to the next, while text that is too narrow can break the reader's rhythm. The ideal line length is often considered to be between 50-75 characters per line.

Hierarchy in typography helps guide the reader's eye through the content. It can be achieved by varying font sizes, weights, and styles. For example, headings are often larger and bolder than body text, helping to break up the content and indicate importance.

Whitespace, or the empty space around text, plays a significant role in readability. Adequate whitespace helps prevent text from feeling cramped and overwhelming. It also allows readers to focus on one section at a time.

Responsive typography ensures that text remains readable on all devices. Media queries can be used to adjust font sizes and line heights based on screen size. For example:

css
Copy code
```css
body {
    font-size: 16px;
    line-height: 1.5;
}

@media (max-width: 600px) {
    body {
        font-size: 14px;
```

```
        line-height: 1.6;
    }
}
```

Pairing fonts effectively involves combining different typefaces that complement each other. A common practice is to use a sans-serif font for headings and a serif font for body text. Tools like Google Fonts provide recommendations for font pairings.

Custom fonts can add a unique touch to a design but should be used sparingly. Overuse of different fonts can make a design look chaotic and unprofessional. Limiting the number of fonts to two or three helps maintain a cohesive look.

Kerning and tracking adjust the spacing between individual letters and groups of letters, respectively. Proper kerning ensures that each letter is visually balanced, while appropriate tracking improves the overall readability of a block of text.

Typography in UI design also involves considering accessibility. Ensuring sufficient contrast between text and background colors, providing options to adjust font sizes, and using accessible fonts all contribute to a more inclusive design.

Typography is a powerful tool in UI/UX design. By carefully selecting and arranging type, designers can enhance readability, convey the right tone, and create a visually appealing and effective user interface.

Iconography and Imagery

Iconography and imagery are vital components of visual design, providing visual cues and enhancing the user experience by conveying information quickly and effectively.

Icons are simplified graphical representations of concepts or actions. They should be easily recognizable and universally understood. Using standard icons for common actions like "save," "edit," or "delete" helps users quickly understand the interface.

When designing custom icons, consistency is key. Icons should follow a consistent style, including line weight, color, and size. This creates a cohesive look and ensures that icons blend seamlessly with the overall design.

Icons should be scalable to different sizes without losing clarity. Vector graphics, such as SVG, are ideal for this purpose because they can be resized without losing quality. Here is an example of SVG code for an icon:

html
Copy code
```
<svg width="24" height="24" viewBox="0 0 24 24" fill="none"
xmlns="http://www.w3.org/2000/svg">
```

```
    <path d="M12 2C6.48 2 2 6.48 2 12s4.48 10 10 10 10-4.48 10-
10S17.52 2 12 2zm0 18c-4.41 0-8-3.59-8-8s3.59-8 8-8 8 3.59 8 8-3.59
8-8 8z" fill="#000"/>
</svg>
```

Imagery includes photos, illustrations, and other visual elements that support the content. High-quality images can enhance the appeal of a design and convey messages more powerfully than text alone.

Selecting appropriate imagery involves considering the target audience and the message being conveyed. For example, using images of people can create an emotional connection, while technical illustrations might be more suitable for instructional content.

Images should be optimized for web use to ensure fast loading times. This involves compressing images without compromising quality and using responsive image techniques to serve different image sizes based on the user's device.

Alt text for images is crucial for accessibility. It provides a text description of the image for screen readers, ensuring that visually impaired users can understand the content. Here's an example of an image tag with alt text:

html
Copy code
```
<img src="image.jpg" alt="A descriptive text of the image">
```

Integrating imagery with other design elements requires careful consideration of layout and whitespace. Images should complement the content and not overwhelm the design. Using grids can help align images with text and other elements, creating a balanced and harmonious layout.

Consistent use of imagery helps reinforce brand identity. Establishing guidelines for image style, color treatment, and subject matter ensures that all images used in the design support the overall brand message.

Stock photos can be useful but should be chosen carefully to avoid clichés and generic imagery. Custom photos and illustrations often provide a more unique and authentic touch to the design.

Hover effects on images and icons can provide interactive feedback to users. For example, changing the color or adding a shadow on hover can indicate that an element is clickable, enhancing usability.

Iconography and imagery, when used effectively, can greatly enhance the visual appeal and usability of a design. By following best practices in consistency, optimization, and accessibility, designers can create a more engaging and effective user experience.

Space and Layout

Space and layout are fundamental aspects of visual design, determining how elements are arranged on the screen and how users interact with them.

Whitespace, also known as negative space, refers to the empty areas between design elements. It's a powerful tool for creating a clean and organized layout, improving readability, and focusing user attention on key elements.

A well-structured layout provides a clear visual hierarchy, guiding users through the content in a logical and intuitive manner. This can be achieved by varying the size, color, and placement of elements to indicate their importance.

Grid systems are commonly used to create structured and balanced layouts. Grids divide the page into columns and rows, providing a framework for aligning elements consistently. Popular grid systems include the 12-column grid for web design and the 8-point grid for spacing.

Responsive layouts adapt to different screen sizes and orientations. Media queries in CSS allow designers to specify different styles for different devices, ensuring a consistent and user-friendly experience across desktops, tablets, and mobile phones. Here's an example of a simple responsive layout using CSS grid:

css
Copy code

```css
.container {
    display: grid;
    grid-template-columns: repeat(auto-fit, minmax(200px, 1fr));
    gap: 16px;
}

.item {
    background-color: #f0f0f0;
    padding: 20px;
}
```

Alignment and spacing are crucial for creating a visually pleasing and functional layout. Consistent margins and padding help separate and group elements, making the design easier to scan and navigate.

Balance in layout design ensures that no single part of the design is too heavy or too light. Symmetrical balance arranges elements evenly around a central axis, creating a formal and stable look. Asymmetrical balance, on the other hand, uses different elements to create a dynamic and interesting composition while maintaining visual harmony.

Proximity in layout design groups related elements together, helping users quickly understand their relationship. For example, placing labels close to form fields makes it clear that they are associated.

Alignment ensures that elements are visually connected and organized. Left, center, right, and justified alignment can be used to create different effects and support the overall design aesthetic.

Hierarchy in layout can be established through the strategic use of size, color, contrast, and typography. Larger and bolder elements attract more attention, while smaller and lighter elements recede into the background.

Consistency in layout design helps create a predictable and user-friendly experience. Repeating patterns, colors, and styles across different pages and sections ensures that users can easily navigate and understand the interface.

Using negative space effectively can enhance the visual appeal and usability of a design. It prevents the layout from feeling cluttered and overwhelming, allowing users to focus on the most important elements.

Space and layout are essential components of effective visual design. By understanding and applying principles of whitespace, grid systems, alignment, and hierarchy, designers can create interfaces that are both aesthetically pleasing and highly functional.

Animation and Interactivity

Animation and interactivity are powerful tools in visual design, adding life and dynamism to the user experience. They can enhance usability, provide feedback, and create engaging and memorable interactions.

Microinteractions are small animations that respond to user actions, providing immediate feedback and enhancing the overall experience. Examples include button presses, hover effects, and loading indicators. These subtle animations help guide users and make the interface feel more responsive.

Transitions and animations can smooth the movement between different states of an interface, such as opening menus, switching tabs, or navigating between pages. Well-designed transitions make these changes feel natural and fluid, improving the user's understanding of the interface.

CSS animations provide a powerful and flexible way to create animations directly in the stylesheet. Keyframes define the start and end points of an animation, and properties like `transition` and `animation` control the timing and behavior. Here's an example of a simple CSS animation:

```css
Copy code
@keyframes fadeIn {
```

```
    from { opacity: 0; }
    to { opacity: 1; }
}

.element {
    animation: fadeIn 1s ease-in-out;
}
```

JavaScript can add more complex interactivity and animations, allowing for dynamic and interactive elements that respond to user input in real-time. Libraries like GSAP (GreenSock Animation Platform) and frameworks like React and Vue provide powerful tools for creating rich, interactive experiences.

Consideration of performance is crucial when implementing animations. Excessive or poorly optimized animations can slow down the interface and create a frustrating user experience. Techniques like hardware acceleration and minimizing the use of JavaScript for animations can help maintain performance.

Animations should enhance the user experience, not distract from it. Overuse of animations can overwhelm users and make the interface feel cluttered. Subtle and purposeful animations are more effective in creating a polished and professional design.

Feedback animations provide users with immediate visual responses to their actions, helping them understand the result of their interactions. For example, a button that changes color or expands when clicked gives clear feedback that the action was registered.

Animated illustrations and graphics can add character and storytelling elements to a design. They can be used to guide users through processes, explain concepts, or simply add a playful touch to the interface.

Loading animations can entertain and inform users while they wait for content to load. Creative loading indicators can make the wait feel shorter and provide a more engaging experience.

Interactivity extends beyond animations to include all forms of user engagement. Interactive elements like forms, buttons, and sliders should be designed to be intuitive and responsive, providing a seamless and enjoyable user experience.

By leveraging animation and interactivity effectively, designers can create more engaging, responsive, and user-friendly interfaces. These elements add a layer of depth and dynamism to the design, enhancing both the visual appeal and functionality of the user experience.

Chapter 8: Interaction Design

Principles of Interaction Design

Interaction design focuses on creating interfaces that facilitate effective and satisfying interactions between users and products. It involves understanding user needs, defining behaviors, and designing elements that enable intuitive and meaningful interactions.

The first principle of interaction design is to keep the user at the center of the process. Understanding user goals, behaviors, and contexts is essential for designing interactions that meet their needs and expectations. User research methods like interviews, surveys, and usability testing provide valuable insights into user behavior and preferences.

Consistency is crucial in interaction design. Consistent use of elements like buttons, icons, and navigation patterns helps users quickly learn and understand the interface. It reduces the cognitive load and makes the interaction experience more predictable and reliable.

Affordances in design indicate how an element can be used. For example, buttons should look clickable, and sliders should indicate that they can be dragged. Clear affordances help users understand possible actions without additional instructions.

Feedback provides users with immediate information about their actions. It can be visual (e.g., a button changing color when clicked), auditory (e.g., a sound indicating a successful action), or haptic (e.g., a vibration on a mobile device). Effective feedback ensures users are aware of the results of their interactions and can correct mistakes if necessary.

Mapping refers to the relationship between controls and their effects. Good mapping ensures that the control layout matches the mental model of the user. For example, a volume control slider should increase volume when moved up and decrease it when moved down.

Constraints guide user behavior by limiting the possible actions. They help prevent errors and streamline the interaction process. For example, a form might restrict the input format for a phone number to avoid invalid entries.

Discoverability ensures that users can easily find and understand available actions. Interfaces should be designed to make key features and functionalities obvious and accessible. Progressive disclosure, where advanced options are hidden until needed, can help manage complexity without overwhelming users.

Efficiency is a key goal in interaction design. Interfaces should be designed to allow users to complete tasks with minimal effort and time. Shortcuts, such as keyboard commands and gesture controls, can enhance efficiency for experienced users.

Flexibility accommodates different user preferences and contexts. Providing multiple ways to achieve the same goal, such as offering both mouse and keyboard navigation, can enhance accessibility and user satisfaction.

Error prevention and recovery are critical aspects of interaction design. Interfaces should be designed to minimize the chances of errors and provide easy ways to correct them when they occur. Clear error messages and undo options help users recover from mistakes without frustration.

The principle of aesthetic and minimalist design emphasizes simplicity. Interfaces should avoid unnecessary elements that do not support user tasks. A clean and uncluttered design enhances usability and focuses attention on essential elements.

User engagement is the ultimate goal of interaction design. Engaging interfaces draw users in, making their interactions enjoyable and meaningful. Gamification elements, such as rewards and progress indicators, can enhance engagement and motivation.

Interaction design is a dynamic and iterative process. Continuous testing, evaluation, and refinement based on user feedback are essential for creating successful interactions. Prototyping and usability testing help identify issues early and ensure that the design meets user needs.

Designing for Touch and Gestures

Designing for touch and gestures involves creating interfaces that are intuitive and responsive to various touch inputs. As touchscreens become increasingly prevalent, understanding how to design for these interactions is crucial.

The first consideration is touch target size. Touch targets, such as buttons and links, should be large enough to be easily tapped with a finger. A minimum size of 44x44 pixels is recommended to accommodate different finger sizes and ensure accurate tapping.

Spacing between touch targets is equally important. Sufficient spacing prevents accidental taps and enhances the overall usability of the interface. Elements should be placed far enough apart to avoid overlapping touch areas.

Gestures are another critical aspect of touch interaction. Common gestures include tapping, swiping, pinching, and dragging. These gestures should be intuitive and consistent across the interface. For example, swiping left or right to navigate between pages should work consistently in all sections of an app.

Feedback for touch interactions is essential for providing a responsive and engaging experience. Visual feedback, such as highlighting a button when tapped, confirms that the action has been registered. Haptic feedback, such as vibrations, can enhance the tactile experience and provide additional confirmation.

Designing for different orientations is necessary for touch interfaces. Users may hold their devices in portrait or landscape mode, and the interface should adapt seamlessly to both orientations. Responsive design techniques ensure that the layout and elements adjust appropriately.

Touch interactions often involve multiple fingers, known as multi-touch gestures. These can include actions like zooming in and out or rotating elements. Designing for multi-touch requires careful consideration of how gestures interact and how they are recognized by the device.

Contextual gestures allow users to perform actions based on the context of their interaction. For example, swiping on a list item might reveal additional options like delete or archive. These contextual gestures should be discoverable and consistent across similar elements.

Accessibility is a crucial consideration in touch and gesture design. Ensuring that touch interactions are accessible to all users, including those with disabilities, is essential. This can involve providing alternative input methods, such as voice commands or physical buttons, and ensuring that touch targets are reachable for users with limited mobility.

Designing for different touch devices involves understanding the capabilities and limitations of each device. Smartphones, tablets, and touchscreen laptops may have different screen sizes, resolutions, and touch sensitivity. Testing on a variety of devices helps ensure a consistent and effective user experience.

Touch gestures should be designed to prevent accidental actions. For example, a swipe gesture should require a deliberate and clear motion to avoid unintended actions. Implementing gesture recognition algorithms that filter out minor and accidental movements can help achieve this.

Custom gestures can enhance the user experience by providing unique and tailored interactions. However, they should be used sparingly and always come with clear instructions to ensure that users understand how to use them.

Designing for touch and gestures is an evolving field, with new technologies and interaction patterns emerging regularly. Staying updated with the latest trends and best practices helps designers create interfaces that are intuitive, responsive, and enjoyable for users.

Motion Design and Microinteractions

Motion design and microinteractions bring interfaces to life, enhancing the user experience by adding visual and interactive elements that respond to user actions and convey information.

Motion design involves creating animations that guide users through the interface, highlight important elements, and provide feedback. It includes transitions, animations, and effects that make interactions feel fluid and natural. Effective motion design can enhance usability, create a sense of continuity, and make the interface more engaging.

Microinteractions are small, focused interactions that occur in response to user actions. They include button presses, hover effects, and loading indicators. These subtle animations provide immediate feedback, making the interface feel more responsive and intuitive.

Transitions help users understand changes in the interface by smoothly animating the movement between different states. For example, a menu that slides in from the side provides a clear indication of its presence and functionality. Well-designed transitions make these changes feel seamless and natural.

Feedback animations provide visual responses to user actions, confirming that the action has been registered. For example, a button that changes color or expands slightly when clicked provides clear feedback that the action was successful. Feedback animations enhance the sense of interactivity and responsiveness.

Animated illustrations and graphics add character and storytelling elements to the interface. They can be used to guide users through processes, explain concepts, or simply add a playful touch to the design. Animated illustrations can make complex information more digestible and engaging.

Loading animations entertain and inform users while they wait for content to load. Creative loading indicators can make the wait feel shorter and provide a more engaging experience. For example, a spinning icon or a progress bar can indicate that the system is working, reducing user frustration.

JavaScript and CSS provide powerful tools for creating motion design and microinteractions. CSS animations and transitions allow for smooth and efficient animations directly in the stylesheet. JavaScript libraries like GSAP (GreenSock Animation Platform) provide advanced animation capabilities for more complex interactions.

Consideration of performance is crucial when implementing motion design. Excessive or poorly optimized animations can slow down the interface and create a frustrating user experience. Techniques like hardware acceleration and minimizing the use of JavaScript for animations can help maintain performance.

Microinteractions should enhance the user experience without distracting from the main tasks. Overuse of animations can overwhelm users and make the interface feel cluttered. Subtle and purposeful microinteractions are more effective in creating a polished and professional design.

Animation timing and easing play a significant role in the feel of motion design. Easing functions control the acceleration and deceleration of animations, making them feel more natural. For example, an ease-in-out easing function can make an animation start slowly, speed up, and then slow down again, mimicking real-world motion.

Responsive design considerations ensure that animations and microinteractions work well on all devices. Media queries can adjust the behavior of animations based on screen size and resolution, ensuring a consistent and enjoyable experience across desktops, tablets, and mobile phones.

Motion design and microinteractions, when used effectively, can greatly enhance the visual appeal and usability of an interface. By adding life and dynamism to the design, they create a more engaging and memorable user experience.

Feedback and Status Indicators

Feedback and status indicators are essential components of interaction design, providing users with real-time information about their actions and the system's state. They help users understand what is happening and confirm that their actions have been registered.

Visual feedback is the most common form of feedback in user interfaces. It includes changes in color, size, or shape of elements in response to user actions. For example, a button that changes color when clicked provides immediate visual confirmation that the action was successful.

Auditory feedback uses sounds to indicate actions and system states. For example, a chime sound when a message is sent or a beep when an error occurs. Auditory feedback can be especially useful for alerting users to important information or errors.

Haptic feedback involves the use of vibrations or other physical sensations to provide feedback. It is commonly used in mobile devices and gaming controllers to enhance the tactile experience. For example, a slight vibration when a button is pressed can provide confirmation that the action was registered.

Status indicators provide information about the current state of the system. They include loading spinners, progress bars, and status messages. These indicators inform users about ongoing processes, such as loading content or processing data, reducing uncertainty and anxiety.

Progress bars are a common form of status indicator, visually representing the completion of a task. They provide users with a clear indication of how much progress has been made and how much is remaining. Progress bars should be accompanied by clear labels indicating the task being performed and the estimated time remaining.

Loading spinners indicate that the system is working and that the user should wait. They are often used for short loading times and should be simple and unobtrusive. If loading times are expected to be longer, a progress bar or detailed status message may be more appropriate.

Status messages provide textual feedback about the system's state. They can indicate success, failure, or ongoing processes. Clear and concise status messages help users understand what is happening and what actions they need to take. For example, a success message like "Your form has been submitted successfully" provides clear feedback that the action was completed.

Notifications are another form of feedback, alerting users to important information or events. They can be visual, auditory, or a combination of both. Notifications should be designed to grab the user's attention without being overly intrusive. They should also provide clear actions that the user can take in response.

Error messages provide feedback about problems or issues that occur during interactions. They should be clear, concise, and helpful, providing users with information about what went wrong and how to fix it. For example, an error message for a failed login attempt might state, "Incorrect password. Please try again."

Interactive feedback, such as real-time validation, provides users with immediate information about the correctness of their inputs. For example, a form field that checks for valid email addresses and provides instant feedback helps users correct errors before submitting the form.

Feedback and status indicators enhance the user experience by providing clarity and reducing uncertainty. By informing users about the results of their actions and the current state of the system, they create a more transparent and satisfying interaction experience.

Affordances and Signifiers

Affordances and signifiers are key concepts in interaction design, helping users understand how to interact with elements in an interface. They play a crucial role in making interfaces intuitive and user-friendly.

Affordances refer to the properties of an object that indicate how it can be used. In the context of user interfaces, affordances suggest possible actions to users. For example, a button's affordance is to be clicked, a slider's affordance is to be dragged, and a text field's affordance is to be typed into.

Signifiers are visual or textual cues that indicate the presence of an affordance. They guide users by highlighting interactive elements and suggesting how to use them. For example, a button's shape, color, and label are signifiers that indicate it can be clicked.

Clear and effective affordances and signifiers are essential for creating intuitive interfaces. They reduce the learning curve and help users quickly understand how to interact with the system. For example, a raised button with a clear label like "Submit" immediately suggests that it can be clicked to perform an action.

Affordances can be explicit or implicit. Explicit affordances are clear and direct, such as a button with a "Click Me" label. Implicit affordances are more subtle, relying on users' prior knowledge and experience. For example, an icon with a downward arrow may imply that clicking it will reveal more options.

Consistency in affordances and signifiers helps users form accurate mental models of the interface. When similar elements behave consistently, users can apply their previous experiences to new interactions. For example, if all buttons in an interface have the same shape and color, users will quickly learn to recognize them as clickable elements.

Visual hierarchy and layout also contribute to effective affordances and signifiers. Elements that are larger, bolder, or positioned prominently are perceived as more important and interactive. For example, a primary call-to-action button might be larger and more brightly colored than secondary buttons.

Interactive feedback reinforces affordances and signifiers by providing real-time confirmation of actions. For example, a button that changes color or provides a tooltip when hovered over reinforces its affordance of being clickable. This feedback helps users understand the results of their interactions and feel confident in their actions.

Signifiers can be enhanced with visual effects such as shadows, gradients, and animations. For example, a button with a drop shadow appears to be raised above the surface, suggesting it can be pressed. A text field with a blinking cursor indicates that it is ready for input.

Textual signifiers, such as labels and instructions, provide additional guidance to users. Clear and concise labels on buttons, form fields, and navigation links help users understand their functions. Instructions and tooltips can provide more detailed guidance for complex interactions.

Affordances and signifiers should also consider accessibility. Ensuring that interactive elements are perceivable and understandable to all users, including those with disabilities, is essential. This can involve using high-contrast colors, providing alternative text for images, and ensuring that interactive elements are keyboard accessible.

Affordances and signifiers are foundational elements of interaction design. By clearly indicating how elements can be used and guiding users through interactions, they create intuitive and user-friendly interfaces. Effective use of affordances and signifiers enhances usability and ensures a satisfying user experience.

Chapter 9: Responsive Design

Importance of Responsive Design

Responsive design is crucial in the modern digital landscape due to the diversity of devices used to access web content. From desktops and laptops to tablets and smartphones, each device has different screen sizes, resolutions, and capabilities. A responsive design ensures that a website or application looks and functions well on all these devices, providing a seamless user experience.

One key aspect of responsive design is the use of flexible layouts. Instead of designing fixed-width layouts, responsive design employs fluid grids that adapt to the screen size. This approach involves using relative units like percentages rather than fixed units like pixels. For example, a container might be defined to occupy 80% of the screen width, allowing it to resize proportionally on different devices.

css
Copy code
```
.container {
  width: 80%;
}
```

Another essential element is the use of flexible images and media. Images and videos should scale according to the container's size, preventing overflow and maintaining their aspect ratio. This can be achieved using CSS properties such as `max-width: 100%` and `height: auto`.

css
Copy code
```
img {
  max-width: 100%;
  height: auto;
}
```

Media queries are another cornerstone of responsive design. They allow designers to apply different styles based on the device's characteristics, such as screen width, height, orientation, and resolution. Media queries can be used to adjust layouts, typography, and other visual elements to ensure optimal usability across various devices.

css
Copy code
```
@media (max-width: 600px) {
  .container {
```

```css
      width: 100%;
  }
}
```

Responsive design also emphasizes the importance of touch-friendly interfaces. As more users access websites via touch devices, ensuring that interactive elements like buttons and links are appropriately sized and spaced is critical. This improves usability and reduces the likelihood of user frustration caused by mis-taps.

Performance optimization is another vital consideration in responsive design. Mobile devices often have limited processing power and slower internet connections compared to desktops. Therefore, optimizing images, minimizing CSS and JavaScript, and leveraging browser caching are essential practices to ensure fast loading times and a smooth user experience.

In conclusion, responsive design is indispensable for creating inclusive, user-friendly digital experiences. It requires a thoughtful approach to layout, media, and performance, ensuring that content is accessible and functional across a wide range of devices.

Designing for Different Devices

Designing for different devices involves understanding the unique characteristics and limitations of each device category. Desktop computers typically have larger screens and more processing power, allowing for more complex and detailed designs. Mobile devices, on the other hand, require simpler, more streamlined interfaces due to their smaller screens and touch-based input methods.

One of the primary challenges in designing for different devices is ensuring consistency while optimizing for each device's capabilities. This involves creating adaptable layouts that can shift and reorganize content based on the screen size. For example, a multi-column layout on a desktop might transform into a single-column layout on a mobile device to improve readability and usability.

css
Copy code
```css
@media (min-width: 768px) {
   .sidebar {
     display: block;
   }
}

@media (max-width: 767px) {
   .sidebar {
     display: none;
   }
}
```

Designing for touch interfaces also requires special consideration. Touch targets, such as buttons and links, need to be large enough to be easily tappable without causing user frustration. The general guideline is to make touch targets at least 44x44 pixels in size, with adequate spacing between them to prevent accidental taps.

Additionally, different devices have different interaction patterns. For instance, desktop users rely on keyboard and mouse interactions, while mobile users primarily use touch gestures. Understanding these differences is crucial for designing intuitive and efficient interfaces. For example, incorporating swipe gestures for navigation on mobile devices can enhance the user experience.

Typography also plays a significant role in responsive design. Font sizes, line heights, and letter spacing need to be adjusted to ensure readability across various screen sizes. On smaller screens, larger font sizes and increased line heights can improve legibility.

```css
Copy code
body {
    font-size: 16px;
    line-height: 1.5;
}

@media (max-width: 600px) {
    body {
        font-size: 14px;
        line-height: 1.6;
    }
}
```

Furthermore, designing for different devices involves considering the context in which the devices are used. Mobile users might be on the go, needing quick access to essential information, while desktop users might be in a more stationary environment, capable of engaging with more detailed content. This context-awareness can guide design decisions, such as prioritizing certain features or content for mobile users.

Finally, testing is a critical part of designing for different devices. Using tools like browser developer tools, device emulators, and real device testing ensures that the design works well across various devices and screen sizes. This iterative testing process helps identify and resolve issues early, leading to a more robust and user-friendly design.

Fluid Grids and Flexible Layouts

Fluid grids and flexible layouts are fundamental concepts in responsive design. Unlike fixed grids, which use fixed pixel values, fluid grids use relative units like percentages to define the width of columns and other elements. This approach allows layouts to adapt to different screen sizes, ensuring a consistent and functional design across devices.

A fluid grid divides the page into a flexible number of columns, which can scale up or down depending on the screen size. For example, a 12-column grid might allocate four columns for a sidebar and eight columns for the main content area on a large screen. On a smaller screen, the sidebar might collapse to the bottom, and the main content area might occupy the full width.

css
Copy code
```css
.container {
  display: flex;
  flex-wrap: wrap;
}

.sidebar {
  flex: 0 0 33.33%;
}

.main-content {
  flex: 0 0 66.67%;
}

@media (max-width: 600px) {
  .sidebar,
  .main-content {
    flex: 0 0 100%;
  }
}
```

Flexible layouts also involve using flexible images and media. By setting the maximum width of images to 100% of their container, they can resize proportionally to fit the available space. This ensures that images do not overflow their containers and maintain their aspect ratio across different devices.

css
Copy code
```css
img {
  max-width: 100%;
  height: auto;
}
```

In addition to flexible grids and images, flexible typography is essential for responsive design. Relative units like em and rem can be used to ensure that text scales appropriately with the screen size. This approach maintains readability and visual hierarchy across devices.

```css
Copy code
body {
  font-size: 1rem;
}

h1 {
  font-size: 2rem;
}

@media (max-width: 600px) {
  body {
    font-size: 0.875rem;
  }

  h1 {
    font-size: 1.75rem;
  }
}
```

The use of CSS flexbox and grid layouts has significantly advanced the implementation of fluid grids and flexible layouts. Flexbox provides a more efficient way to distribute space and align items within a container, making it easier to create responsive designs. Similarly, CSS grid offers a powerful system for defining complex layouts that can adapt to different screen sizes.

```css
Copy code
.container {
  display: grid;
  grid-template-columns: repeat(auto-fit, minmax(200px, 1fr));
  gap: 16px;
}
```

Using these techniques, designers can create layouts that adjust dynamically to the user's device, providing an optimal viewing experience. This approach not only enhances usability but also improves accessibility, ensuring that content is accessible to all users, regardless of the device they are using.

In summary, fluid grids and flexible layouts are essential for creating responsive designs that adapt to various screen sizes. By using relative units, flexible images, and advanced CSS layout techniques, designers can ensure that their designs are both functional and aesthetically pleasing across different devices.

Media Queries and Breakpoints

Media queries and breakpoints are integral components of responsive design, allowing developers to apply different styles based on the characteristics of the user's device. Media queries can target various features, such as screen width, height, resolution, orientation, and more. By defining breakpoints, designers can specify where the layout should change to accommodate different screen sizes.

A common approach is to start with a mobile-first design, which means designing for the smallest screens first and then progressively enhancing the design for larger screens. This approach ensures that the core functionality is accessible on all devices, while additional features and enhancements are added for larger screens.

```css
Copy code
body {
    font-size: 14px;
}

@media (min-width: 600px) {
    body {
        font-size: 16px;
    }
}

@media (min-width: 1024px) {
    body {
        font-size: 18px;
    }
}
```

In this example, the base font size is set for mobile devices, and then increased for tablets and desktops using media queries. The breakpoints at 600px and 1024px define where the font size changes to improve readability on larger screens.

Breakpoints should be chosen based on the content and design, rather than specific devices. While certain device sizes are common, new devices with different screen sizes are constantly being released. By focusing on the content and its requirements, designers can create more flexible and future-proof designs.

css
Copy code

```css
@media (min-width: 480px) {
  /* Styles for small devices */
}

@media (min-width: 768px) {
  /* Styles for medium devices */
}

@media (min-width: 1200px) {
  /* Styles for large devices */
}
```

Media queries can also target other device features, such as orientation. For instance, different styles can be applied when the device is in portrait or landscape mode, ensuring an optimal layout for both orientations.

css
Copy code

```css
@media (orientation: portrait) {
  .container {
    flex-direction: column;
  }
}

@media (orientation: landscape) {
  .container {
    flex-direction: row;
  }
}
```

Responsive images are another area where media queries play a crucial role. The srcset attribute allows developers to specify different image sources for different screen sizes, ensuring that users receive appropriately sized images for their devices.

html
Copy code

```html
<img src="small.jpg" srcset="medium.jpg 600w, large.jpg 1200w"
alt="Responsive Image">
```

In this example, the browser selects the best image source based on the device's screen size and resolution. This approach improves performance by delivering smaller images to mobile devices and higher-resolution images to desktops.

Media queries can also be combined with other CSS features, such as CSS variables and custom properties, to create more dynamic and responsive designs. For example, CSS variables can be defined and modified within media queries to adjust styles based on the screen size.

css
Copy code
```css
:root {
  --primary-color: blue;
}

@media (min-width: 600px) {
  :root {
    --primary-color: green;
  }
}

@media (min-width: 1024px) {
  :root {
    --primary-color: red;
  }
}

button {
  background-color: var(--primary-color);
}
```

In conclusion, media queries and breakpoints are essential tools for creating responsive designs that adapt to various devices and screen sizes. By using media queries to apply different styles based on device characteristics, designers can ensure a consistent and user-friendly experience across all devices.

Adaptive vs. Responsive Design

Adaptive and responsive design are two approaches to creating websites that work well on various devices. While they share the common goal of improving usability across different screen sizes, they employ different strategies to achieve this goal.

Responsive design uses a single flexible layout that adjusts and rearranges content based on the screen size. This approach relies heavily on fluid grids, flexible images, and media queries to create a seamless experience across all devices. The same HTML and CSS are used for all devices, with styles adapting dynamically to the available screen space.

css
Copy code

```css
.container {
  width: 100%;
  max-width: 1200px;
  margin: 0 auto;
  padding: 16px;
}

@media (min-width: 768px) {
  .container {
    padding: 32px;
  }
}
```

Adaptive design, on the other hand, involves creating multiple fixed layouts for different screen sizes. Each layout is tailored to a specific range of screen widths, and the server delivers the appropriate layout based on the device's characteristics. This approach can provide a more optimized experience for each device but requires more development effort and maintenance.

html
Copy code

```html
<link rel="stylesheet" media="screen and (max-width: 480px)" href="small.css">
<link rel="stylesheet" media="screen and (min-width: 481px) and (max-width: 1024px)" href="medium.css">
<link rel="stylesheet" media="screen and (min-width: 1025px)" href="large.css">
```

One advantage of responsive design is its flexibility. Since the layout adjusts fluidly to any screen size, it can accommodate new devices with different dimensions without requiring significant changes. This makes responsive design more future-proof and easier to maintain.

Adaptive design, however, can offer better performance on each device. By serving only the necessary resources for the specific device, adaptive designs can reduce load times and improve user experience. This approach can be particularly beneficial for sites with complex functionality or large amounts of data.

The choice between adaptive and responsive design depends on various factors, including the project's requirements, target audience, and available resources. For many projects, a responsive design is sufficient and offers a good balance of flexibility and performance. However, for complex applications or sites with specific performance needs, an adaptive approach might be more appropriate.

In some cases, a hybrid approach that combines elements of both responsive and adaptive design can be used. For example, a responsive design might be implemented with certain adaptive elements, such as serving different images or media files based on the device.

html
Copy code

```html
<picture>
    <source media="(max-width: 600px)" srcset="small.jpg">
    <source media="(max-width: 1200px)" srcset="medium.jpg">
    <img src="large.jpg" alt="Adaptive Image">
</picture>
```

In conclusion, both adaptive and responsive design have their strengths and weaknesses. Understanding the differences and knowing when to apply each approach can help designers and developers create more effective and user-friendly websites. The choice should be guided by the specific needs of the project and the preferences of the target audience.

Chapter 10: Accessibility in UI/UX

Understanding Accessibility

Accessibility in UI/UX design is the practice of creating digital content and interfaces that are usable by all people, regardless of their abilities or disabilities. This includes ensuring that websites and applications can be navigated and understood by individuals with visual, auditory, motor, or cognitive impairments.

One of the primary principles of accessibility is perceivability. This means that users must be able to perceive the information being presented. For users with visual impairments, this might involve providing text alternatives for images, videos, and other non-text content. Screen readers can then interpret these text alternatives, allowing visually impaired users to understand the content.

html
Copy code
```html
<img src="logo.png" alt="Company Logo">
```

Operability is another key principle. Users must be able to navigate and interact with a website or application using various input methods, such as a keyboard, mouse, or assistive devices. Ensuring that all interactive elements, such as buttons and links, can be accessed and operated using a keyboard is crucial for users with motor impairments.

html
Copy code
```html
<a href="#main-content" class="skip-link">Skip to main content</a>
```

Understandability involves making content clear and easy to comprehend. This includes using simple language, providing instructions and feedback, and ensuring that the design is consistent and predictable. For users with cognitive impairments, clear and straightforward content can significantly enhance usability.

Robustness refers to the ability of content to be reliably interpreted by various technologies including assistive technologies. This means using standard HTML elements and attributes correctly and ensuring that web pages are compatible with current and future user agents including browsers and assistive technologies.

html
Copy code
```html
<button type="submit">Submit</button>
```

Accessibility is not just about compliance with legal standards; it also enhances the overall user experience. By designing for accessibility, we create more inclusive products that benefit a wider range of users, including those with temporary disabilities, such as a broken arm, or situational limitations, like bright sunlight.

Incorporating accessibility into the design process from the beginning is more effective than trying to retrofit accessibility into an existing product. This proactive approach helps identify potential barriers early and integrate accessible solutions seamlessly.

Accessibility testing is a critical component of the design process. Using tools like screen readers, keyboard-only navigation, and automated accessibility checkers can help identify and address issues. Manual testing with users who have disabilities can also provide valuable insights and ensure that the product meets their needs.

In summary, understanding and implementing accessibility in UI/UX design is essential for creating inclusive, user-friendly digital experiences. By following accessibility principles and incorporating best practices, designers can ensure that their products are usable by all people, regardless of their abilities.

Legal and Ethical Considerations

Legal and ethical considerations play a significant role in accessibility in UI/UX design. Various laws and regulations mandate accessibility standards to ensure that digital content is accessible to individuals with disabilities. Understanding and complying with these laws is not only a legal obligation but also an ethical responsibility.

In many countries, laws such as the Americans with Disabilities Act (ADA) in the United States, the Equality Act in the United Kingdom, and the Web Content Accessibility Guidelines (WCAG) set by the World Wide Web Consortium (W3C) provide frameworks for accessibility. These laws require that websites and digital content be accessible to individuals with disabilities, ensuring equal access to information and services.

The ADA, for example, requires that public accommodations, including websites, be accessible to people with disabilities. Failure to comply with the ADA can result in legal actions and penalties. Similarly, the Equality Act in the UK mandates that organizations make reasonable adjustments to ensure accessibility for individuals with disabilities.

The WCAG guidelines provide a comprehensive set of recommendations for making web content more accessible. These guidelines are organized into four principles: Perceivable, Operable, Understandable, and Robust (POUR). Each principle contains specific guidelines and success criteria, which are categorized into three levels of conformance: A, AA, and AAA.

html
Copy code

```html
<!-- Example of WCAG conformance -->
<nav aria-label="Main Navigation">
  <ul>
```

```
    <li><a href="#home">Home</a></li>
    <li><a href="#about">About</a></li>
    <li><a href="#services">Services</a></li>
    <li><a href="#contact">Contact</a></li>
  </ul>
</nav>
```

Ethically, designing for accessibility is about inclusivity and social responsibility. By creating accessible digital experiences, designers and developers ensure that everyone, regardless of their abilities, can participate in the digital world. This inclusive approach not only benefits individuals with disabilities but also enhances the overall user experience for all users.

Accessibility also has business benefits. An accessible website can reach a broader audience, including individuals with disabilities, elderly users, and those with temporary impairments. This can lead to increased engagement, customer satisfaction, and loyalty. Additionally, accessible websites are often better optimized for search engines, improving their visibility and ranking.

Moreover, accessibility can drive innovation. Designing for diverse user needs can lead to the development of new technologies and solutions that benefit a wide range of users. For example, voice recognition and text-to-speech technologies, initially developed for individuals with disabilities, have become mainstream features used by many.

Ensuring accessibility requires a commitment from the entire organization. It involves ongoing education and training, incorporating accessibility into the design and development process, and regularly testing and evaluating products for accessibility. Creating an inclusive culture that values diversity and accessibility is essential for long-term success.

In conclusion, legal and ethical considerations are fundamental to accessibility in UI/UX design. By understanding and complying with accessibility laws and guidelines, and embracing an inclusive approach, designers and developers can create digital experiences that are accessible to all users, ensuring equal access and opportunity.

Designing for Disabilities

Designing for disabilities involves creating digital content and interfaces that accommodate a wide range of physical, sensory, and cognitive impairments. By considering the diverse needs of users with disabilities, designers can ensure that their products are inclusive and accessible.

Visual impairments, including blindness, low vision, and color blindness, require specific design considerations. For blind users, providing text alternatives for non-text content, such as images and videos, is crucial. Screen readers can interpret these text alternatives, allowing users to understand the content. Ensuring that all interactive elements, such as buttons and links, are accessible via keyboard is also important.

html
Copy code

```html
<img src="chart.png" alt="Sales chart showing an increase in revenue
over the last quarter">
```

For users with low vision, designers should ensure that text is readable and scalable. This can be achieved by using relative units for font sizes and providing sufficient color contrast between text and background. Users should be able to zoom in on content without losing functionality or readability.

CSS
Copy code

```css
body {
  font-size: 1rem;
  line-height: 1.5;
}

@media (min-width: 768px) {
  body {
    font-size: 1.125rem;
  }
}
```

Color blindness requires careful use of color in design. Designers should avoid relying solely on color to convey information and should use text labels, patterns, or icons to differentiate elements. Tools like color contrast checkers can help ensure that color combinations are distinguishable for users with color blindness.

html
Copy code

```html
<div class="status status-success">Success</div>
<div class="status status-error">Error</div>
```

CSS
Copy code

```css
.status-success {
  color: #28a745;
}

.status-error {
  color: #dc3545;
}
```

Auditory impairments, including deafness and hard of hearing, also require specific design considerations. Providing captions and transcripts for audio and video content ensures that users can access the information. Interactive elements should also provide visual feedback to indicate changes in state or completion of actions.

html
Copy code

```
<video controls>
  <source src="video.mp4" type="video/mp4">
  <track kind="captions" src="captions.vtt" srclang="en" label="English">
</video>
```

Motor impairments, including limited dexterity and mobility, require interfaces that are easy to navigate and operate. Designers should ensure that all interactive elements are accessible via keyboard and provide sufficient spacing to prevent accidental activation. Implementing touch-friendly interfaces with appropriately sized touch targets is also important for users with motor impairments.

css
Copy code

```
button {
  padding: 12px 24px;
  font-size: 1rem;
}
```

Cognitive impairments, including learning disabilities and memory issues, require clear and simple design. Using plain language, breaking information into manageable chunks, and providing consistent navigation can improve usability for users with cognitive impairments. Designers should also avoid using complex layouts and interactions that might confuse users.

Providing multiple ways to access information and complete tasks can accommodate a variety of disabilities. For example, offering both text and graphical representations of information can benefit users with different impairments. Similarly, providing options for users to customize their experience, such as adjusting text size or color schemes, can enhance accessibility.

In conclusion, designing for disabilities involves understanding and addressing the diverse needs of users with various impairments. By following accessibility best practices and incorporating inclusive design principles, designers can create digital experiences that are accessible to all users, ensuring equal access and usability.

Accessible Design Practices

Accessible design practices are essential for creating digital content and interfaces that are usable by all people, including those with disabilities. These practices ensure that websites and applications meet the diverse needs of users and comply with accessibility standards.

One of the fundamental practices is providing text alternatives for non-text content. This includes images, videos, and interactive elements. Text alternatives allow screen readers to interpret and convey the information to users with visual impairments. For example, using the `alt` attribute for images provides a description that screen readers can read aloud.

html
Copy code
```html
<img src="team.jpg" alt="Photo of the company team">
```

Keyboard accessibility is another crucial practice. All interactive elements, such as links, buttons, and form controls, should be operable using a keyboard. This ensures that users with motor impairments who cannot use a mouse can navigate and interact with the content. Using semantic HTML elements, such as `<button>` and `<a>`, and managing focus states effectively are key aspects of keyboard accessibility.

html
Copy code
```html
<a href="#main-content" class="skip-link">Skip to main content</a>
```

Ensuring sufficient color contrast between text and background is vital for users with visual impairments, including color blindness and low vision. The WCAG guidelines recommend a contrast ratio of at least 4.5:1 for normal text and 3:1 for large text. Tools like color contrast checkers can help designers verify that their color choices meet these requirements.

css
Copy code
```css
body {
   color: #333;
   background-color: #fff;
}

a {
   color: #007bff;
}
```

Using descriptive link text improves accessibility by providing context for users navigating with screen readers. Instead of using generic phrases like "click here," designers should use meaningful text that describes the link's destination or purpose.

html
Copy code

```html
<a href="report.pdf">Download the annual report</a>
```

Forms should be designed with accessibility in mind. This includes providing clear labels for all form controls, grouping related controls using fieldsets and legends, and providing instructions and error messages that are easy to understand. Ensuring that form controls are large enough to be easily tappable on touch devices is also important.

html
Copy code

```html
<form>
  <label for="name">Name:</label>
  <input type="text" id="name" name="name">

  <label for="email">Email:</label>
  <input type="email" id="email" name="email">

  <button type="submit">Submit</button>
</form>
```

Responsive design practices are also essential for accessibility. Ensuring that content adapts to different screen sizes and orientations makes it accessible to users on various devices, including smartphones, tablets, and desktops. This involves using fluid grids, flexible images, and media queries to create a layout that works well across different screen sizes.

css
Copy code

```css
.container {
  display: flex;
  flex-wrap: wrap;
}

@media (max-width: 600px) {
  .container {
    flex-direction: column;
  }
}
```

Providing captions and transcripts for multimedia content, such as videos and audio files, ensures that users with auditory impairments can access the information. Captions provide a text representation of the audio content, while transcripts offer a full text version that can be read at the user's convenience.

html
Copy code
```html
<video controls>
  <source src="presentation.mp4" type="video/mp4">
  <track kind="captions" src="captions.vtt" srclang="en" label="English">
</video>
```

In conclusion, accessible design practices are essential for creating inclusive digital experiences. By providing text alternatives, ensuring keyboard accessibility, maintaining sufficient color contrast, using descriptive link text, designing accessible forms, implementing responsive design, and offering captions and transcripts, designers can ensure that their products are usable by all people, regardless of their abilities.

Testing for Accessibility

Testing for accessibility is a critical part of the design and development process. It involves evaluating digital content and interfaces to ensure they meet accessibility standards and are usable by individuals with disabilities. Several methods and tools can be used to test for accessibility, each providing unique insights and identifying different types of issues.

Automated accessibility testing tools are a good starting point for identifying common accessibility issues. Tools like Axe, Lighthouse, and WAVE can scan web pages and generate reports highlighting potential problems, such as missing alt text, insufficient color contrast, and improper heading structure. These tools can be integrated into the development workflow to catch issues early and ensure continuous compliance.

sh
Copy code
```sh
# Example of running Lighthouse accessibility audit
lighthouse https://example.com --only-categories=accessibility
```

Manual testing is essential for identifying issues that automated tools might miss. This involves using the website or application as a user with disabilities would, navigating with a keyboard, screen reader, or other assistive technologies. Manual testing helps uncover usability issues and provides a deeper understanding of the user experience.

Keyboard testing involves navigating through the site using only the keyboard. Testers should ensure that all interactive elements are focusable and operable, and that the focus order is logical and intuitive. Users should be able to access all functionality without relying on a mouse.

Screen reader testing involves using a screen reader to navigate and interact with the content. Popular screen readers include JAWS, NVDA, and VoiceOver. Testers should ensure that all content is accessible, including images, links, form controls, and multimedia. They should also verify that ARIA (Accessible Rich Internet Applications) roles and attributes are used correctly.

Color contrast testing ensures that text and interactive elements have sufficient contrast with their backgrounds. This can be done using color contrast analyzers, which calculate the contrast ratio and compare it against WCAG standards. Ensuring sufficient contrast improves readability for users with visual impairments.

User testing with individuals who have disabilities provides valuable feedback and insights. By involving users with various impairments in the testing process, designers can identify real-world issues and understand how to improve the user experience. This approach helps ensure that the product meets the needs of all users.

Accessibility audits conducted by third-party experts can provide an in-depth evaluation of the website or application. These audits typically involve a combination of automated and manual testing, followed by a detailed report outlining the findings and recommendations for improvement.

Regular testing and monitoring are essential to maintain accessibility over time. As new content and features are added, ongoing testing ensures that accessibility standards are upheld. Integrating accessibility checks into the development and deployment processes helps catch issues early and ensures continuous compliance.

In conclusion, testing for accessibility is a vital part of creating inclusive digital experiences. By using automated tools, conducting manual testing, involving users with disabilities, and performing regular audits, designers and developers can identify and address accessibility issues, ensuring that their products are usable by all people.

Chapter 10: User Interface Patterns

Common UI Patterns

User interface (UI) patterns are reusable solutions to common design problems. They provide a consistent and efficient way to solve recurring design challenges, improving usability and enhancing the user experience. Common UI patterns include navigation menus, form designs, content organization, and interaction feedback.

Navigation menus are essential for guiding users through a website or application. Common navigation patterns include top navigation bars, side menus, and hamburger menus. Top navigation bars are typically used for primary navigation and are placed at the top of the page. Side menus, often found on the left or right side, can provide additional navigation options or secondary content.

html

```
<nav>
  <ul>
    <li><a href="#home">Home</a></li>
    <li><a href="#about">About</a></li>
    <li><a href="#services">Services</a></li>
    <li><a href="#contact">Contact</a></li>
  </ul>
</nav>
```

Form designs are another common UI pattern. Forms are used to collect user input, such as login information, contact details, and feedback. Effective form design includes clear labels, input validation, and feedback for errors and successful submissions. Grouping related fields, using placeholders, and providing hints can improve the user experience.

html

```
<form>
  <label for="name">Name:</label>
  <input type="text" id="name" name="name">

  <label for="email">Email:</label>
  <input type="email" id="email" name="email">

  <button type="submit">Submit</button>
</form>
```

Content organization patterns help structure information in a way that is easy to understand and navigate. Common patterns include card layouts, grids, and lists. Card layouts present content in visually distinct containers, making it easy to scan and digest information. Grids provide a structured layout for organizing multiple elements, while lists are useful for presenting sequential information.

html

```
<div class="card">
  <h2>Title</h2>
  <p>Content goes here...</p>
</div>
```

Interaction feedback is crucial for informing users about the results of their actions. Common feedback patterns include loading indicators, success messages, and error alerts. Loading indicators, such as spinners and progress bars, inform users that a process is ongoing. Success messages confirm that an action was completed successfully, while error alerts provide information about what went wrong and how to fix it.

html
Copy code
```
<div       class="alert       alert-success">Your       submission       was
successful!</div>
<div class="alert alert-error">There  was  an  error  processing  your
request.</div>
```

Modal dialogs are a common pattern for drawing attention to important information or requiring user input before proceeding. Modals typically overlay the main content and can be used for confirmations, alerts, or forms. Ensuring that modals are accessible and easy to close is important for a positive user experience.

html
Copy code
```
<div class="modal">
  <div class="modal-content">
    <span class="close">&times;</span>
    <p>Modal content goes here...</p>
  </div>
</div>
```

Breadcrumbs provide a way for users to navigate back to previous sections or the homepage. This pattern is especially useful for deep or hierarchical navigation structures. Breadcrumbs improve navigation by showing users their current location within the site hierarchy.

html
Copy code
```
<nav aria-label="breadcrumb">
  <ol>
    <li><a href="#home">Home</a></li>
    <li><a href="#section">Section</a></li>
    <li><a href="#subsection">Subsection</a></li>
  </ol>
</nav>
```

Tabs are a UI pattern used to organize content into different sections within the same page. Tabs allow users to switch between sections without leaving the page, improving navigation and content organization. Ensuring that tabs are clearly labeled and indicate the active tab is important for usability.

html
Copy code

```html
<div class="tabs">
  <button class="tablink active">Tab 1</button>
  <button class="tablink">Tab 2</button>
  <button class="tablink">Tab 3</button>
</div>

<div class="tabcontent">
  <p>Content for Tab 1...</p>
</div>
```

In conclusion, common UI patterns provide reusable solutions to frequent design challenges, enhancing usability and consistency. By implementing navigation menus, form designs, content organization patterns, interaction feedback, modal dialogs, breadcrumbs, and tabs, designers can create user-friendly interfaces that improve the overall user experience.

Chapter 11: User Interface Patterns

Common UI Patterns

User Interface (UI) patterns are standardized solutions to common design problems, making them a crucial component in creating intuitive and effective interfaces. These patterns help designers solve usability issues by providing proven frameworks that enhance the user experience.

UI patterns offer consistency across applications, aiding users in understanding and navigating different interfaces with ease. Some common UI patterns include:

Navigation Patterns

Navigation patterns are essential for guiding users through an application or website. Common navigation patterns include:

1. Top Navigation Bar: Positioned at the top of the page, this bar typically contains links to the main sections of a site or app. It's a straightforward way to provide primary navigation options.

2. Side Navigation: A vertical menu on the side of the page, often collapsible. This pattern is beneficial for applications with numerous sections, as it can organize content effectively without overwhelming the user.

3. Breadcrumbs: These are small text paths, usually at the top of the page, showing the user's location within the site hierarchy. They provide an easy way to navigate back to previous sections.

4. Dropdown Menus: These menus reveal additional options when clicked or hovered over. Dropdowns help to keep the interface clean by hiding secondary options until needed.

5. Mega Menus: A type of dropdown that displays multiple options in a large panel, useful for websites with extensive categories, such as e-commerce sites.

6. Tab Navigation: Tabs allow users to switch between different views or sections within the same page. This is useful for organizing related content into digestible sections.

7. Pagination: This pattern breaks down content into discrete pages, typically used in lists or search results, making large sets of data easier to navigate.

8. Infinite Scroll: Instead of breaking content into pages, infinite scroll loads more content as the user scrolls down. This is common in social media feeds and some e-commerce sites.

These navigation patterns improve usability by helping users find information quickly and efficiently.

Form Design Patterns

Forms are a fundamental element of user interaction, allowing users to input and submit data. Effective form design patterns enhance usability and completion rates. Key form design patterns include:

1. Single-Column Layout: Arranging form fields in a single column is the most straightforward and user-friendly approach, as it aligns with the natural reading flow.

2. Grouped Fields: Grouping related fields together with clear headings improves comprehension and navigation. For example, separating personal information from payment details in a checkout form.

3. Inline Validation: Providing real-time feedback on user input helps prevent errors and reduces frustration. For instance, indicating whether a password meets the required criteria as the user types.

4. Progressive Disclosure: Breaking long forms into multiple steps, revealing only relevant sections as needed. This technique makes forms less daunting and improves focus.

5. Pre-filled Fields: Using available data to pre-fill fields reduces the user's effort. For example, auto-filling a user's city based on their postal code.

6. Placeholder Text: Using placeholder text within input fields to provide examples or instructions. This can guide users without cluttering the interface.

7. Toggle Elements: Using switches, checkboxes, or radio buttons for binary choices simplifies decision-making and data entry.

8. Clear Call-to-Action Buttons: Ensuring submit buttons are prominently displayed and labeled with clear, action-oriented text (e.g., "Submit," "Sign Up").

9. Confirmation Messages: Providing feedback upon form submission, such as success messages or error notifications, helps users understand the outcome of their actions.

Effective form design patterns reduce user frustration and increase the likelihood of successful form completion.

Content Presentation Patterns

Content presentation patterns ensure that information is displayed in an accessible and engaging manner. Key content presentation patterns include:

1. Card Layouts: Using cards to group related information visually. This pattern is highly flexible and works well for displaying products, articles, or user profiles.

2. Grid Systems: Implementing a grid system to organize content in a structured manner, making it easier to scan and read.

3. Lists: Displaying information in a list format, either ordered or unordered, for straightforward content organization.

4. Accordions: Collapsible panels that expand to reveal more information. This pattern is useful for organizing large amounts of content without overwhelming the user.

5. Sliders/Carousels: Displaying a series of items or images in a horizontal or vertical slider. This pattern is effective for showcasing featured content or image galleries.

6. Modal Windows: Pop-up windows that focus the user's attention on a specific task or piece of information, such as a login form or a larger view of an image.

7. Tooltips: Small hover-activated boxes that provide additional information about an element, such as explaining the purpose of a button or link.

8. Tables: Organizing data into rows and columns for easy comparison and analysis. Tables are particularly useful for displaying quantitative information.

9. Infinite Scroll: Continuously loading more content as the user scrolls down the page, ideal for content-heavy applications like social media feeds.

10. Masonry Layout: Arranging elements in an optimal position based on available vertical space, often used for image galleries or portfolios.

These content presentation patterns enhance readability and engagement by organizing information in a user-friendly manner.

Patterns for Mobile Interfaces

Designing for mobile interfaces requires unique patterns that cater to smaller screens and touch interactions. Common mobile UI patterns include:

1. Bottom Navigation Bar: Placing primary navigation options at the bottom of the screen within easy reach of the user's thumb.

2. Hamburger Menu: A collapsible menu that reveals navigation options when tapped. This pattern saves screen space while still providing access to additional content.

3. Floating Action Button (FAB): A prominent button that floats above the interface, usually in the bottom right corner, for primary actions like adding a new item or composing a message.

4. Swipe Gestures: Implementing swipe actions for navigation, such as swiping left or right to switch between tabs or delete an item.

5. Pull-to-Refresh: Allowing users to refresh content by pulling down the screen, commonly used in social media apps and email clients.

6. Tap to Expand: Enabling users to tap on an element to expand it for more details, useful for lists or card interfaces.

7. Sticky Headers: Keeping headers fixed at the top of the screen as users scroll, ensuring important navigation options remain accessible.

8. Scrollable Tabs: Using horizontal scrolling for tabs, allowing users to access more sections without crowding the screen.

9. Bottom Sheets: Partial modal windows that slide up from the bottom of the screen, providing additional options or information without navigating away from the current view.

10. Gesture Navigation: Utilizing gestures like pinching, spreading, and long-pressing to enhance navigation and interaction.

These mobile UI patterns optimize the user experience by making the most of limited screen space and leveraging touch interactions.

Navigation Patterns

Navigation patterns are crucial for guiding users through an application or website, ensuring they can easily find the information or features they need. Effective navigation design enhances usability and user satisfaction. Some common navigation patterns include:

1. Top Navigation Bar: A horizontal bar at the top of the page that contains links to the main sections of a site or app. This pattern is widely used due to its simplicity and visibility.

2. Side Navigation: A vertical menu positioned on the side of the page, often collapsible. This pattern is useful for applications with extensive sections or categories, as it can display many options without overwhelming the user.

3. Breadcrumbs: A trail of links that shows the user's current location within the site hierarchy. Breadcrumbs improve navigation by allowing users to backtrack easily.

4. Dropdown Menus: Menus that reveal additional options when clicked or hovered over. Dropdowns are efficient for presenting secondary options without cluttering the main interface.

5. Mega Menus: Large panels that display multiple options in a dropdown format. Mega menus are ideal for websites with extensive categories, providing a comprehensive overview at a glance.

6. Tab Navigation: Tabs allow users to switch between different views or sections within the same page. This pattern is effective for organizing related content into manageable sections.

7. Pagination: Dividing content into separate pages, typically used in lists or search results. Pagination makes large sets of data easier to navigate.

8. Infinite Scroll: Continuously loading more content as the user scrolls down. Infinite scroll is common in social media feeds and e-commerce sites, offering a seamless browsing experience.

9. Contextual Navigation: Providing navigation options that are relevant to the current context or content. This pattern helps users find related information without navigating away from their current view.

10. Footer Navigation: A set of links placed at the bottom of the page, often used for secondary or less frequently accessed options like legal information and contact details.

These navigation patterns enhance usability by providing clear and efficient paths for users to follow, ensuring they can find what they need quickly and easily.

Chapter 12: User Experience Metrics and Analytics

Key UX Metrics

User Experience (UX) metrics are essential for evaluating the effectiveness of a design and understanding how users interact with a product. Key UX metrics include:

1. Task Success Rate: The percentage of users who successfully complete a task. This metric helps identify usability issues and measure the effectiveness of design changes.

2. Time on Task: The amount of time it takes for users to complete a task. Shorter times generally indicate more efficient and intuitive designs.

3. Error Rate: The frequency of errors made by users while interacting with the product. High error rates can highlight problematic areas in the design that need improvement.

4. Abandonment Rate: The percentage of users who start but do not complete a task. High abandonment rates may indicate a frustrating or confusing user experience.

5. System Usability Scale (SUS): A widely used questionnaire that provides a subjective measure of usability. The SUS score helps gauge overall user satisfaction with the product.

6. Net Promoter Score (NPS): Measures users' likelihood to recommend the product to others. NPS is a strong indicator of user satisfaction and loyalty.

7. Customer Satisfaction (CSAT): A survey metric that asks users to rate their satisfaction with the product. CSAT scores provide direct feedback on user satisfaction.

8. Retention Rate: The percentage of users who continue to use the product over time. High retention rates suggest a positive user experience and value.

9. Conversion Rate: The percentage of users who complete a desired action, such as making a purchase or signing up for a newsletter. This metric is crucial for evaluating the effectiveness of call-to-actions and overall design.

10. Click-Through Rate (CTR): The percentage of users who click on a specific link or button. CTR helps assess the effectiveness of design elements and content placement.

By monitoring these UX metrics, designers can make data-driven decisions to enhance the user experience and achieve business goals.

Analyzing User Behavior

Understanding user behavior is crucial for improving the user experience and making informed design decisions. Analyzing user behavior involves examining how users interact with a product, identifying patterns, and uncovering insights. Key methods for analyzing user behavior include:

1. Heatmaps: Visual representations of where users click, scroll, and hover on a page. Heatmaps help identify popular areas and potential issues, such as elements that are overlooked or misunderstood.

2. Session Recordings: Videos of user sessions that capture their interactions with the product. Session recordings provide a detailed view of user behavior, highlighting pain points and areas of confusion.

3. Clickstream Analysis: Tracking the sequence of pages or actions taken by users during their visit. Clickstream analysis helps understand user journeys and identify common paths and drop-off points.

4. A/B Testing: Comparing two versions of a design to see which performs better. A/B testing helps optimize design elements by testing variations and measuring their impact on user behavior.

5. User Surveys: Collecting feedback directly from users through surveys. Surveys can provide qualitative insights into user preferences, motivations, and pain points.

6. Funnel Analysis: Analyzing the steps users take to complete a specific goal, such as making a purchase. Funnel analysis helps identify where users drop off and why.

7. User Testing: Observing users as they interact with the product in a controlled environment. User testing provides direct insights into usability issues and user satisfaction.

8. Behavioral Analytics Tools: Using tools like Google Analytics, Mixpanel, or Hotjar to track and analyze user interactions. These tools provide comprehensive data on user behavior and engagement.

9. Cohort Analysis: Segmenting users into groups based on shared characteristics or behaviors. Cohort analysis helps understand how different user groups interact with the product over time.

10. Path Analysis: Examining the paths users take to complete tasks or reach goals. Path analysis helps identify common routes and potential obstacles.

By analyzing user behavior, designers can gain valuable insights into how users interact with the product, identify areas for improvement, and make informed design decisions.

Tools for UX Analytics

UX analytics tools are essential for collecting, analyzing, and interpreting data on user behavior and experience. These tools provide valuable insights that help designers optimize their products. Some popular UX analytics tools include:

1. Google Analytics: A comprehensive web analytics tool that tracks user interactions, traffic sources, and conversion rates. Google Analytics provides detailed reports and insights into user behavior.

2. Hotjar: A tool that offers heatmaps, session recordings, and user surveys. Hotjar helps visualize user interactions and gather direct feedback from users.

3. Mixpanel: An advanced analytics platform that tracks user actions and events. Mixpanel provides insights into user behavior, engagement, and retention.

4. Crazy Egg: A tool that provides heatmaps, scroll maps, and click reports. Crazy Egg helps identify popular areas and potential issues in the design.

5. FullStory: A session recording tool that captures user interactions in detail. FullStory provides insights into user behavior and helps identify pain points and usability issues.

6. Optimizely: An A/B testing platform that allows designers to experiment with different design variations. Optimizely helps optimize design elements based on user feedback and behavior.

7. Adobe Analytics: A powerful analytics tool that provides detailed insights into user behavior and engagement. Adobe Analytics helps track and analyze user interactions across multiple channels.

8. Pendo: A tool that combines product analytics, user feedback, and in-app messaging. Pendo helps understand user behavior and improve the product experience.

9. Amplitude: An analytics platform that focuses on product usage and user engagement. Amplitude provides insights into user behavior, retention, and conversion.

10. UsabilityHub: A user testing tool that offers remote testing and user feedback. UsabilityHub helps gather insights into user preferences and usability issues.

By using these UX analytics tools, designers can gather comprehensive data on user behavior, identify areas for improvement, and make data-driven decisions to enhance the user experience.

Measuring Usability

Measuring usability is critical for evaluating the effectiveness of a design and identifying areas for improvement. Usability metrics provide insights into how easily users can interact with a product. Key methods for measuring usability include:

1. Usability Testing: Observing users as they complete tasks in a controlled environment. Usability testing provides direct insights into user interactions, pain points, and satisfaction.

2. System Usability Scale (SUS): A standardized questionnaire that assesses the overall usability of a product. The SUS score helps gauge user satisfaction and identify usability issues.

3. Task Success Rate: The percentage of users who successfully complete a task. This metric indicates how well the design supports users in achieving their goals.

4. Time on Task: The amount of time it takes for users to complete a task. Shorter times generally indicate more efficient and intuitive designs.

5. Error Rate: The frequency of errors made by users while interacting with the product. High error rates highlight problematic areas in the design.

6. Abandonment Rate: The percentage of users who start but do not complete a task. High abandonment rates may indicate a frustrating or confusing user experience.

7. Think-Aloud Protocol: Asking users to verbalize their thoughts while interacting with the product. This method provides qualitative insights into user behavior and decision-making.

8. Heuristic Evaluation: Experts evaluate the design against established usability principles (heuristics). This method helps identify potential usability issues based on best practices.

9. Cognitive Walkthrough: Experts simulate a user's thought process to identify usability issues. This method focuses on understanding how users learn and navigate the interface.

10. Remote Usability Testing: Conducting usability tests with users in their natural environment. Remote testing provides insights into real-world interactions and usability.

By measuring usability through these methods, designers can identify strengths and weaknesses in the design, make data-driven improvements, and enhance the overall user experience.

Improving UX with Data

Data-driven design involves using quantitative and qualitative data to inform design decisions and improve the user experience. By leveraging data, designers can identify areas for improvement, optimize user interactions, and achieve business goals. Key strategies for improving UX with data include:

1. Setting Clear Goals: Defining specific, measurable goals for the user experience. Clear goals help focus data collection and analysis efforts.

2. Collecting Comprehensive Data: Using a combination of quantitative and qualitative methods to gather data on user behavior and preferences. This includes analytics tools, user surveys, and usability testing.

3. Analyzing User Behavior: Examining data to identify patterns, pain points, and opportunities for improvement. Tools like heatmaps, session recordings, and funnel analysis provide valuable insights.

4. A/B Testing: Experimenting with different design variations to see which performs better. A/B testing helps optimize design elements and improve user interactions.

5. User Feedback: Gathering feedback directly from users through surveys, interviews, and usability tests. User feedback provides qualitative insights into user preferences and pain points.

6. Iterative Design: Continuously refining the design based on data and user feedback. Iterative design helps ensure the product meets user needs and expectations.

7. Prioritizing Improvements: Using data to prioritize design improvements based on their potential impact on the user experience. Focus on high-impact areas first.

8. Monitoring Key Metrics: Regularly tracking key UX metrics, such as task success rate, time on task, and user satisfaction. Monitoring metrics helps measure the effectiveness of design changes.

9. Collaborative Design: Involving stakeholders, including designers, developers, and product managers, in the data analysis and decision-making process. Collaboration ensures a holistic approach to improving the user experience.

10. Continuous Learning: Staying informed about the latest UX research, trends, and best practices. Continuous learning helps designers apply new insights and techniques to their work.

By using data to inform design decisions, designers can create more effective, user-centered products that meet user needs and achieve business goals.

Chapter 13: UI/UX for Different Platforms

Web Design Considerations

Web design plays a crucial role in ensuring a seamless user experience across various devices and browsers. Key considerations include responsiveness, loading speed, accessibility, and SEO.

Responsive design ensures that a website adjusts smoothly to different screen sizes, providing an optimal viewing experience. This can be achieved through flexible grids, fluid layouts, and media queries.

Loading speed is vital for user retention. Techniques to improve speed include optimizing images, minifying CSS and JavaScript, leveraging browser caching, and using content delivery networks (CDNs).

Accessibility ensures that websites are usable by people with disabilities. This involves following WCAG guidelines, providing text alternatives for non-text content, ensuring keyboard navigability, and using ARIA roles and properties.

SEO helps in ranking higher on search engines, driving organic traffic. Key aspects include optimizing meta tags, using semantic HTML, improving page speed, and creating high-quality content.

Cross-browser compatibility is also essential. This involves testing and ensuring that the website functions correctly across different browsers, handling CSS and JavaScript quirks specific to each browser.

Usability testing is critical to identify and resolve issues that real users might face. This involves conducting A/B testing, heatmaps, and user feedback sessions.

Security is another important aspect. Implementing HTTPS, protecting against XSS and SQL injection, and regular security audits are necessary to safeguard user data.

Web design should also consider mobile-first approaches. This involves designing the mobile version first and then enhancing it for larger screens, ensuring a seamless experience across all devices.

Using a content management system (CMS) can streamline the web design process, allowing non-technical users to manage content easily. Popular CMS options include WordPress, Joomla, and Drupal.

Integration with third-party tools and APIs can enhance website functionality. This includes integrating social media platforms, payment gateways, and analytics tools.

Mobile Design Considerations

Mobile design requires a unique approach, focusing on touch interactions, limited screen space, and varied device capabilities.

Touch interactions are fundamental in mobile design. This includes designing for gestures like swipes, taps, and pinches. Ensuring that touch targets are large enough and spaced adequately is crucial for a seamless experience.

Limited screen space necessitates prioritizing content. Designers must ensure that essential information and actions are easily accessible. This often involves simplifying navigation and using expandable elements like accordions.

Performance is critical on mobile devices. Optimizing performance involves reducing image sizes, minimizing the use of heavy animations, and leveraging lazy loading techniques.

Designing for different screen sizes and resolutions requires a responsive approach. Media queries, flexible grids, and vector graphics can help in adapting the design to various devices.

Offline functionality is a valuable feature in mobile apps. This can be achieved using service workers, which allow caching of essential resources, enabling the app to function without an internet connection.

Integration with device-specific features can enhance user experience. This includes using GPS for location-based services, accelerometers for motion detection, and cameras for AR experiences.

Push notifications can engage users by providing timely updates and information. However, they should be used judiciously to avoid overwhelming users.

Usability testing on actual devices is crucial. This helps in identifying issues that might not be apparent in emulators or simulators, ensuring a smooth experience across different devices.

Accessibility is equally important in mobile design. This involves providing text alternatives for visual content, ensuring voiceover compatibility, and designing for color contrast.

App store optimization (ASO) is vital for discoverability. This involves optimizing the app's title, description, keywords, and visuals to improve its ranking in app stores.

Designing for Wearables

Designing for wearables presents unique challenges and opportunities. Wearables include smartwatches, fitness trackers, and AR glasses, each requiring specific design considerations.

Smartwatches have small screens and limited input methods. Designers must prioritize essential information and interactions, using simple and clear visuals. Voice commands and gestures can be leveraged to enhance usability.

Fitness trackers focus on health and activity data. Design should emphasize clarity and ease of access to real-time data. Integrating with health apps and providing actionable insights based on data can add value.

AR glasses offer immersive experiences, blending digital and real-world elements. Design should consider spatial awareness, ensuring that digital elements do not obstruct the user's view. Intuitive interaction methods like gaze control and voice commands are essential.

Battery life is a critical consideration for wearables. Optimizing performance and minimizing background processes can extend battery life, enhancing the user experience.

Contextual awareness is a key feature of wearables. Designing for context involves understanding the user's environment and providing relevant information and actions. For example, a fitness tracker might suggest a workout based on the user's location and activity history.

Notifications on wearables should be concise and actionable. Given the limited screen space, designers should prioritize brevity and clarity, ensuring that notifications can be quickly understood and acted upon.

Integration with other devices and platforms can enhance the functionality of wearables. For instance, a smartwatch might control smart home devices or interact with a smartphone app.

Privacy and security are paramount in wearable design. Ensuring data encryption, providing clear privacy policies, and allowing users to control data sharing are essential for building trust.

User testing is crucial for wearables, given their unique form factors and use cases. Real-world testing helps in identifying usability issues and refining the design for optimal performance.

UI/UX for Virtual Reality

Virtual reality (VR) offers immersive experiences, requiring distinct design principles compared to traditional platforms.

Spatial design is fundamental in VR. Designers must consider the 3D space, ensuring that virtual environments are navigable and intuitive. This involves understanding depth, scale, and user perspective.

Interaction methods in VR include gaze control, hand tracking, and controllers. Designing intuitive interactions involves leveraging natural gestures and minimizing the learning curve for users.

Comfort is a major concern in VR. Reducing motion sickness involves maintaining a stable frame rate, minimizing rapid movements, and providing visual references to ground the user in the virtual environment.

Sound design enhances immersion in VR. Spatial audio can provide cues about the environment, helping users navigate and interact with virtual elements. Using realistic and high-quality audio contributes to a more engaging experience.

Feedback is essential in VR interactions. Providing visual, auditory, and haptic feedback helps users understand the outcomes of their actions, improving the overall experience.

Usability testing in VR is critical. Testing with real users helps in identifying issues related to comfort, interaction, and navigation, ensuring a smooth and enjoyable experience.

Accessibility in VR involves designing for users with different abilities. This includes providing options for different interaction methods, adjusting settings for comfort, and ensuring that virtual environments are inclusive.

Optimizing performance is crucial for VR. High frame rates, minimal latency, and efficient resource management contribute to a smooth and immersive experience.

Narrative and storytelling play a significant role in VR. Designing compelling narratives involves understanding user agency and creating interactive elements that drive the story forward.

Cross-Platform Design Strategies

Cross-platform design aims to provide a consistent user experience across different devices and platforms.

Consistency is key in cross-platform design. Ensuring that design elements, interactions, and branding are uniform across platforms helps in building a cohesive experience.

Design systems can streamline cross-platform design. A design system includes reusable components, guidelines, and assets that ensure consistency and efficiency in the design process.

Responsive design principles apply to cross-platform design. This involves creating flexible layouts that adapt to different screen sizes and orientations, ensuring a seamless experience across devices.

Performance optimization is crucial for cross-platform apps. Techniques like code splitting, lazy loading, and efficient resource management help in delivering a smooth experience on various platforms.

Platform-specific adaptations enhance the user experience. While maintaining overall consistency, designers should leverage platform-specific features and conventions to provide a familiar and optimized experience.

User feedback is valuable in refining cross-platform designs. Conducting usability testing on different devices helps in identifying and addressing issues specific to each platform.

Chapter 14: Advanced UI/UX Techniques

Persuasive Design

Persuasive design aims to influence user behavior through psychological principles and design techniques.

The Fogg Behavior Model is a key framework in persuasive design. It posits that behavior is a function of motivation, ability, and triggers. Designing for behavior change involves understanding these elements and crafting experiences that align with user motivations and abilities.

Social proof is a powerful persuasive tool. Displaying testimonials, reviews, and user generated content can build trust and influence user decisions.

Scarcity creates a sense of urgency. Limited-time offers, countdown timers, and highlighting low stock levels can drive users to take action.

Personalization enhances the persuasive power of design. Tailoring content recommendations, and interactions to individual users increases relevance and engagement.

Gamification involves applying game elements to non-game contexts. Techniques like points, badges, and leaderboards can motivate users to engage more deeply with the product.

Emotional design leverages users' emotions to create a connection. Using visuals narratives, and interactions that evoke positive emotions can enhance user engagement and satisfaction.

Cognitive biases influence decision-making. Understanding and leveraging biases like anchoring, loss aversion, and the decoy effect can guide users towards desired actions.

Emotional Design

Emotional design focuses on creating products that elicit positive emotional responses from users.

The three levels of emotional design, as proposed by Don Norman, include visceral behavioral, and reflective. Visceral design concerns the immediate visual impact, behavioral design focuses on usability and functionality, and reflective design involves the user' personal and cultural connections to the product.

Color plays a significant role in emotional design. Different colors evoke different emotions and understanding color psychology helps in creating desired emotional responses.

Typography contributes to the overall tone of the design. Choosing the right fonts and typographic hierarchy can influence readability and the emotional impact of the content.

Imagery and visuals are powerful emotional triggers. Using high-quality images, illustrations, and icons that align with the brand's personality can create a strong emotional connection.

Microinteractions add delight to the user experience. Small animations, sounds, and haptic feedback can enhance the emotional appeal of interactions.

Personalization in emotional design involves tailoring the experience to individual users. This can be achieved through customized content, recommendations, and adaptive interfaces.

Gamification in UX

Gamification involves incorporating game elements into non-game contexts to enhance user engagement and motivation.

Points and rewards provide immediate feedback and recognition for user actions. This can motivate users to complete tasks and engage more deeply with the product.

Badges and achievements recognize and celebrate user accomplishments. They provide a sense of progression and can drive users to explore and achieve more.

Leaderboards introduce a competitive element. They can motivate users to improve their performance and compare themselves with others.

Challenges and quests add a sense of adventure. Structuring tasks as challenges or quests can make the experience more engaging and enjoyable.

Designing for Behavior Change

Designing for behavior change involves creating experiences that guide users towards desired behaviors through psychological principles and design techniques.

The COM-B model is a framework for understanding behavior change. It posits that behavior is a result of capability, opportunity, and motivation. Designing for behavior change involves addressing these components.

Nudging is a technique to influence behavior subtly. Small design changes, like default options and visual cues, can guide users towards desired actions without restricting their choices.

Habits are a key focus in behavior change design. Creating experiences that support habit formation involves providing cues, simplifying actions, and offering rewards.

Incorporating AI and Machine Learning

Incorporating AI and machine learning into UI/UX design can enhance personalization, automation, and user insights.

Personalization is a major benefit of AI. Machine learning algorithms can analyze user data to provide tailored recommendations, content, and experiences.

Automation can improve efficiency and convenience. AI-powered chatbots, virtual assistants, and predictive text can streamline interactions and reduce user effort.

User insights from AI can inform design decisions. Analyzing user behavior and preferences can help in identifying pain points, optimizing the experience, and predicting future needs.

Ethical considerations are important in AI-driven design. Ensuring transparency, fairness, and privacy in AI interactions builds trust and protects user interests.

Chapter 15: Agile and Lean UX

Principles of Agile UX

Agile UX is a methodology that integrates user experience design into Agile software development processes. The key principle is to ensure that UX design is not an afterthought but a continuous part of the development cycle. This integration helps in creating products that are both functional and user-friendly.

Agile UX emphasizes collaboration between designers, developers, and stakeholders. This collaboration ensures that user feedback is incorporated at every stage of the development process. Regular communication and iterative design are crucial components of Agile UX.

One of the main goals of Agile UX is to create a seamless user experience. This is achieved by continuously testing and refining the product based on user feedback. This approach helps in identifying and addressing usability issues early in the development process.

In Agile UX, user stories are used to define the features and functionalities of the product. These user stories are created based on the needs and requirements of the end-users. This ensures that the product is designed with the user in mind.

The iterative nature of Agile UX allows for flexibility in the design process. Designers can make changes and improvements based on user feedback and testing results. This helps in creating a product that meets the needs of the users and adapts to changing requirements.

Agile UX also focuses on creating a Minimum Viable Product (MVP). The MVP is a version of the product with the minimum features necessary to satisfy early adopters. This approach allows for early testing and feedback, which is crucial for refining the product.

Prototyping is an essential part of Agile UX. Designers create prototypes to visualize and test the design before it is fully developed. This helps in identifying and addressing any design issues early in the process.

Agile UX promotes a user-centered design approach. This means that the needs and preferences of the users are prioritized throughout the development process. User research and testing are crucial components of this approach.

Another key principle of Agile UX is to embrace change. The iterative nature of Agile UX allows for changes and improvements to be made based on user feedback and testing results. This helps in creating a product that meets the needs of the users and adapts to changing requirements.

In Agile UX, designers work closely with developers to ensure that the design is implemented correctly. This collaboration helps in creating a seamless user experience and ensures that the product meets the design specifications.

Lean UX Methodology

Lean UX is a methodology that focuses on minimizing waste and maximizing value in the design process. It emphasizes collaboration, rapid prototyping, and iterative design to create products that meet the needs of the users.

One of the main goals of Lean UX is to reduce the time and resources spent on design activities that do not add value. This is achieved by focusing on the essential features and functionalities of the product and eliminating unnecessary elements.

Lean UX promotes a user-centered design approach. This means that the needs and preferences of the users are prioritized throughout the development process. User research and testing are crucial components of this approach.

In Lean UX, designers work closely with developers and stakeholders to ensure that the product meets the needs of the users. This collaboration helps in creating a seamless user experience and ensures that the product meets the design specifications.

Rapid prototyping is an essential part of Lean UX. Designers create prototypes to visualize and test the design before it is fully developed. This helps in identifying and addressing any design issues early in the process.

Lean UX also emphasizes the importance of continuous feedback and improvement. This is achieved by testing the product with users and incorporating their feedback into the design. This iterative approach helps in creating a product that meets the needs of the users.

In Lean UX, user stories are used to define the features and functionalities of the product. These user stories are created based on the needs and requirements of the end-users. This ensures that the product is designed with the user in mind.

The iterative nature of Lean UX allows for flexibility in the design process. Designers can make changes and improvements based on user feedback and testing results. This helps in creating a product that meets the needs of the users and adapts to changing requirements.

Lean UX also focuses on creating a Minimum Viable Product (MVP). The MVP is a version of the product with the minimum features necessary to satisfy early adopters. This approach allows for early testing and feedback, which is crucial for refining the product.

Another key principle of Lean UX is to embrace change. The iterative nature of Lean UX allows for changes and improvements to be made based on user feedback and testing results. This helps in creating a product that meets the needs of the users and adapts to changing requirements.

Collaborative Design

Collaborative design is a key aspect of both Agile and Lean UX methodologies. It involves the active participation of designers, developers, stakeholders, and users in the design process. This collaboration ensures that the product is designed with a comprehensive understanding of user needs and technical constraints.

The first step in collaborative design is to establish a shared vision and goals for the project. This involves defining the problem to be solved, the target audience, and the desired outcomes. By aligning the team's goals, collaborative design fosters a sense of ownership and commitment among all participants.

Workshops and brainstorming sessions are common practices in collaborative design. These sessions provide a platform for team members to share ideas, discuss potential solutions, and identify challenges. This open communication helps in generating diverse ideas and ensures that all perspectives are considered.

User involvement is crucial in collaborative design. By engaging users early and often, designers can gather valuable insights and feedback that inform the design process. Techniques such as user interviews, surveys, and usability testing are used to understand user needs and preferences.

Collaborative design also involves creating shared artifacts, such as wireframes, prototypes, and design documents. These artifacts serve as a reference for the team and help in maintaining consistency and clarity throughout the project. Tools like collaborative whiteboards and design software facilitate real-time collaboration and feedback.

Cross-functional teams are a hallmark of collaborative design. By bringing together individuals with diverse skills and expertise, these teams can address various aspects of the design, from user experience and interface design to technical implementation and business strategy. This holistic approach ensures that the product is well-rounded and meets user needs effectively.

Iterative feedback loops are essential in collaborative design. By continuously testing and refining the product based on user feedback, the team can identify and address issues early in the process. This iterative approach helps in creating a product that is both functional and user-friendly.

Collaboration tools play a significant role in facilitating collaborative design. Tools like Slack, Trello, and Figma enable real-time communication, task management, and design collaboration. These tools help in keeping the team aligned and ensure that everyone is on the same page.

In collaborative design, decision-making is a shared responsibility. By involving all team members in the decision-making process, the team can leverage diverse perspectives and expertise. This democratic approach helps in making informed decisions that benefit the project as a whole.

Collaborative design also emphasizes the importance of a supportive team culture. By fostering an environment of trust, respect, and open communication, the team can work together more effectively and overcome challenges. This positive culture helps in maintaining team morale and motivation throughout the project.

Rapid Prototyping

Rapid prototyping is an essential practice in Agile and Lean UX methodologies. It involves quickly creating low-fidelity versions of a product to test ideas, gather feedback, and refine designs. This iterative approach helps in identifying and addressing design issues early in the process, reducing the risk of costly changes later on.

The first step in rapid prototyping is to define the key features and functionalities of the product. This involves creating user stories or scenarios that outline the desired user interactions and outcomes. By focusing on the most critical aspects of the design, the team can create prototypes that effectively address user needs.

Low-fidelity prototypes, such as sketches or wireframes, are typically used in the initial stages of rapid prototyping. These simple, visual representations of the design allow for quick exploration of different ideas and concepts. Tools like paper and pencil, whiteboards, or digital wireframing software can be used to create these prototypes.

Once a low-fidelity prototype is created, it is tested with users to gather feedback. This feedback helps in identifying usability issues, understanding user preferences, and validating design assumptions. Techniques such as usability testing, A/B testing, and heuristic evaluations are commonly used to gather user feedback.

Based on the feedback received, the prototype is refined and iterated upon. This involves making changes to the design, adding new features, and addressing any issues identified during testing. This iterative process continues until the design meets the desired user experience and functionality.

High-fidelity prototypes, which are more detailed and interactive, are created in later stages of rapid prototyping. These prototypes closely resemble the final product and allow for more comprehensive testing of the design. Tools like Adobe XD, Sketch, and InVision are commonly used to create high-fidelity prototypes.

Rapid prototyping also involves collaboration between designers, developers, and stakeholders. By working together, the team can ensure that the prototype accurately reflects the design vision and is feasible to implement. This collaboration helps in identifying technical constraints and addressing any potential issues early in the process.

Documentation is an important aspect of rapid prototyping. By documenting the design decisions, user feedback, and changes made during the prototyping process, the team can maintain a clear record of the project's progress. This documentation helps in maintaining consistency and provides a reference for future iterations.

Incorporating user feedback is crucial in rapid prototyping. By continuously testing and refining the prototype based on user feedback, the team can create a product that effectively meets user needs and preferences. This user-centered approach helps in ensuring the success of the final product.

Rapid prototyping also allows for flexibility in the design process. By quickly exploring different ideas and concepts, the team can adapt to changing requirements and make informed design decisions. This flexibility helps in creating a product that is both innovative and user-friendly.

Continuous Improvement

Continuous improvement is a core principle of Agile and Lean UX methodologies. It involves the ongoing refinement and enhancement of the product based on user feedback, testing results, and changing requirements. This iterative approach helps in creating a product that evolves to meet the needs of the users and remains competitive in the market.

The first step in continuous improvement is to establish a baseline for the product's performance. This involves measuring key metrics such as usability, user satisfaction, and engagement. These metrics serve as a reference point for evaluating the effectiveness of design changes and improvements.

User feedback is a crucial component of continuous improvement. By regularly gathering feedback from users, the team can identify areas for improvement and understand user needs and preferences. Techniques such as surveys, interviews, and usability testing are commonly used to gather user feedback.

Based on the feedback received, the team makes iterative changes to the design. This involves refining existing features, adding new functionalities, and addressing any usability issues. This iterative process continues until the design meets the desired user experience and functionality.

Collaboration is essential in continuous improvement. By working together, designers, developers, and stakeholders can ensure that the product evolves in a way that meets user needs and technical constraints. This collaboration helps in identifying potential issues early and making informed design decisions.

Regular testing is a key aspect of continuous improvement. By continuously testing the product with users, the team can validate design changes and identify any issues that may arise. Techniques such as A/B testing, usability testing, and heuristic evaluations are commonly used to test the product.

Documentation is important in continuous improvement. By documenting the design changes, testing results, and user feedback, the team can maintain a clear record of the project's progress. This documentation helps in maintaining consistency and provides a reference for future iterations.

Flexibility is crucial in continuous improvement. By being open to change and willing to adapt, the team can respond to new requirements and user feedback effectively. This flexibility helps in creating a product that remains relevant and meets the evolving needs of the users.

Continuous improvement also involves learning from past experiences. By analyzing the successes and failures of previous iterations, the team can identify best practices and avoid repeating mistakes. This learning process helps in enhancing the overall quality of the product.

Another key aspect of continuous improvement is to stay updated with industry trends and advancements. By keeping up with the latest developments in design and technology, the team can incorporate new ideas and techniques into the product. This helps in creating a product that is innovative and competitive.

In conclusion, continuous improvement is a vital practice in Agile and Lean UX methodologies. By focusing on iterative refinement, user feedback, and collaboration, the team can create a product that evolves to meet user needs and remains competitive in the market. This approach helps in ensuring the success and longevity of the product.

Chapter 16: Case Studies in UI/UX Design

Successful UI/UX Projects

Successful UI/UX projects are often characterized by a user-centered design approach, effective collaboration, and iterative refinement. These projects demonstrate how thoughtful design and continuous improvement can lead to products that are both functional and user-friendly.

One example of a successful UI/UX project is the redesign of Airbnb. The company focused on improving the user experience by conducting extensive user research and testing. They identified key pain points in the booking process and made iterative changes to address these issues. The result was a more intuitive and seamless user experience that significantly increased user engagement and satisfaction.

Another notable example is the redesign of the Dropbox website. Dropbox aimed to simplify the user interface and enhance usability. They conducted user interviews and usability testing to gather feedback and identify areas for improvement. The redesigned website featured a cleaner layout, improved navigation, and clearer calls to action. This led to increased user adoption and retention.

The success of Slack is also a testament to effective UI/UX design. Slack focused on creating a user-friendly interface that facilitated collaboration and communication. They conducted extensive user research and testing to understand the needs and preferences of their users. The result was a highly intuitive and engaging platform that became a preferred tool for team communication.

Google Maps is another example of a successful UI/UX project. The design team focused on providing a seamless and intuitive user experience by continuously testing and refining the product. They incorporated user feedback and made iterative changes to improve usability and functionality. This user-centered approach helped Google Maps become the go-to navigation tool for millions of users worldwide.

Spotify's UI/UX design is also worth mentioning. The company focused on creating a personalized and engaging user experience. They conducted user research to understand listening habits and preferences. The result was a highly intuitive and customizable interface that enhanced user satisfaction and retention.

Apple's iOS design is a prime example of successful UI/UX. Apple prioritizes simplicity, consistency, and user-centered design. They conduct extensive user research and testing to ensure that their products meet the needs and preferences of their users. The result is a highly intuitive and seamless user experience that has set a benchmark in the industry.

The redesign of BBC's website is another notable example. The BBC focused on improving the user experience by conducting user research and usability testing. They identified key pain points and made iterative changes to address these issues. The redesigned website featured a cleaner layout, improved navigation, and a more intuitive user interface. This led to increased user engagement and satisfaction.

Trello's success is also attributed to effective UI/UX design. Trello focused on creating a user-friendly and intuitive interface that facilitated task management and collaboration. They conducted user research and testing to understand the needs and preferences of their users. The result was a highly engaging and easy-to-use platform that became a preferred tool for project management.

The redesign of The New York Times website is another example of successful UI/UX. The company aimed to improve the reading experience by conducting user research and testing. They identified key pain points and made iterative changes to address these issues. The redesigned website featured a cleaner layout, improved navigation, and a more intuitive user interface. This led to increased user engagement and satisfaction.

In conclusion, successful UI/UX projects are characterized by a user-centered design approach, effective collaboration, and iterative refinement. By focusing on the needs and preferences of the users, conducting extensive research and testing, and continuously improving the product, these projects have achieved significant success and set a benchmark in the industry.

Lessons from Failed Projects

Failed UI/UX projects often provide valuable insights and lessons that can help in avoiding similar pitfalls in future projects. These failures are usually characterized by a lack of user-centered design, poor communication, and insufficient testing.

One example of a failed UI/UX project is the redesign of the healthcare.gov website. The website faced numerous usability issues, technical glitches, and performance problems at launch. The primary lesson from this failure is the importance of thorough testing and iterative refinement. The lack of adequate testing and the rush to meet the launch deadline resulted in a poor user experience and significant backlash.

Another notable example is the launch of the Windows 8 operating system. The drastic change in the user interface, with the introduction of the tile-based Start screen, confused and frustrated many users. The lesson here is the importance of understanding user needs and preferences. A sudden and significant change in the user interface without proper user research and testing can lead to a negative user experience.

Google Wave is another example of a failed UI/UX project. Despite its innovative features, the complexity of the interface and lack of clear use cases led to its downfall. The key takeaway from this failure is the importance of simplicity and clarity in UI/UX design. A complex and confusing interface can deter users, regardless of the innovative features.

The launch of Snapchat's redesign in 2018 also faced significant backlash. The redesign changed the layout and navigation of the app, confusing and frustrating many users. The lesson from this failure is the importance of gradual and user-tested changes. A sudden and significant change in the user interface without proper user feedback can lead to a negative user experience.

Myspace's decline is another example of a failed UI/UX project. The cluttered interface, lack of personalization, and slow performance contributed to its downfall. The lesson here is the importance of a clean, personalized, and responsive user interface. A cluttered and slow interface can drive users away.

Yahoo's redesign in 2013 also faced significant criticism. The redesign focused on aesthetics but neglected usability and performance. The lesson from this failure is the importance of balancing aesthetics with usability and performance. A visually appealing design that lacks usability and performance can lead to a negative user experience.

The failure of Microsoft Zune is another example. The device faced usability issues and lacked key features that were present in competing products. The lesson here is the importance of thorough user research and competitive analysis. Understanding user needs and preferences, and offering features that meet those needs, is crucial for success.

Blackberry's decline is also a notable example. The company failed to adapt to the changing user preferences for touchscreens and app ecosystems. The lesson from this failure is the importance of staying updated with industry trends and user preferences. Failing to adapt to changing trends can lead to obsolescence.

The launch of the Facebook Home app also faced significant backlash. The app replaced the Android home screen, confusing and frustrating many users. The lesson here is the importance of respecting existing user behaviors and preferences. Forcing a drastic change in user behavior without proper user research and testing can lead to a negative user experience.

In conclusion, failed UI/UX projects provide valuable lessons on the importance of user-centered design, thorough testing, clear communication, and staying updated with industry trends. By learning from these failures, designers can avoid similar pitfalls and create products that meet user needs and preferences effectively.

Redesigning Popular Products

Redesigning popular products is a challenging task that requires careful consideration of existing user behaviors, preferences, and expectations. The goal is to improve the user experience while maintaining the core features and functionalities that users love.

One example of a successful redesign is the transformation of Instagram's interface in 2016. The redesign introduced a cleaner and more modern look while maintaining the app's core functionalities. The key to this success was the gradual and iterative approach. Instagram tested various design elements with users and incorporated their feedback before the official launch.

Another notable example is the redesign of Microsoft's Office suite. The introduction of the Fluent Design System in Office 365 aimed to create a more consistent and intuitive user experience across devices. Microsoft conducted extensive user research and testing to ensure that the redesign met the needs and preferences of their diverse user base.

The redesign of LinkedIn in 2020 is also worth mentioning. LinkedIn focused on improving the user experience by simplifying the interface, enhancing navigation, and introducing new features. The redesign was based on user feedback and iterative testing, ensuring that the changes were well-received by the users.

Spotify's redesign in 2019 is another example of a successful transformation. The redesign focused on improving usability and personalization. Spotify conducted user research to understand listening habits and preferences. The result was a more intuitive and personalized interface that enhanced user satisfaction and retention.

The redesign of Dropbox's website is also a notable example. Dropbox aimed to simplify the user interface and enhance usability. They conducted user interviews and usability testing to gather feedback and identify areas for improvement. The redesigned website featured a cleaner layout, improved navigation, and clearer calls to action. This led to increased user adoption and retention.

Facebook's timeline redesign in 2011 is another example. The introduction of the timeline feature aimed to create a more engaging and organized user experience. Facebook conducted extensive user research and testing to ensure that the redesign met the needs and preferences of their users. The result was a highly engaging and organized interface that increased user engagement.

The redesign of Google's Gmail in 2018 is also worth mentioning. The redesign introduced a cleaner and more modern look while maintaining the core functionalities of the email service. Google conducted extensive user research and testing to ensure that the redesign met the needs and preferences of their users. The result was a more intuitive and user-friendly interface that increased user satisfaction.

The redesign of Apple's iOS 7 is another notable example. The introduction of a flatter and more modern design aimed to create a more intuitive and seamless user experience. Apple conducted extensive user research and testing to ensure that the redesign met the needs and preferences of their users. The result was a highly intuitive and seamless interface that set a benchmark in the industry.

The redesign of the BBC's website is also worth mentioning. The BBC focused on improving the user experience by conducting user research and usability testing. They identified key pain points and made iterative changes to address these issues. The redesigned website featured a cleaner layout, improved navigation, and a more intuitive user interface. This led to increased user engagement and satisfaction.

In conclusion, redesigning popular products requires a careful and user-centered approach. By conducting extensive user research, iterative testing, and gradual implementation, designers can create a redesigned product that meets user needs and preferences while maintaining the core features and functionalities that users love.

Innovative UI/UX Solutions

Innovative UI/UX solutions often involve the use of new technologies, design trends, and user-centered approaches to create unique and engaging user experiences. These solutions push the boundaries of traditional design and provide valuable insights into the future of UI/UX design.

One example of an innovative UI/UX solution is the use of virtual reality (VR) in user experience design. VR provides an immersive and interactive experience that can be used for various applications, such as gaming, education, and training. The use of VR in UI/UX design requires a deep understanding of user interactions in a 3D space and the creation of intuitive and engaging interfaces.

Another notable example is the use of artificial intelligence (AI) and machine learning in UI/UX design. AI can be used to create personalized and adaptive user experiences by analyzing user behavior and preferences. For example, AI-powered chatbots can provide personalized customer support, while machine learning algorithms can recommend content based on user interests.

Voice user interfaces (VUIs) are also an example of innovative UI/UX solutions. VUIs, such as Amazon's Alexa and Google Assistant, provide a hands-free and intuitive way for users to interact with devices and services. Designing VUIs requires a deep understanding of natural language processing and user interactions with voice commands.

The use of augmented reality (AR) in UI/UX design is another example of innovation. AR overlays digital content onto the real world, providing an interactive and engaging experience. AR can be used for various applications, such as navigation, gaming, and retail. Designing AR interfaces requires a deep understanding of user interactions with both digital and physical environments.

Microinteractions are also an example of innovative UI/UX solutions. Microinteractions are small, subtle animations or design elements that enhance the user experience by providing feedback, guidance, or engagement. For example, a "like" animation on social media or a loading spinner on a website are microinteractions that improve the overall user experience.

Another example of innovation in UI/UX design is the use of dark mode. Dark mode provides a visually appealing and comfortable user experience, especially in low-light environments. Designing for dark mode requires careful consideration of color contrast, readability, and user preferences.

Progressive web apps (PWAs) are also an example of innovative UI/UX solutions. PWAs combine the best features of web and mobile apps, providing a seamless and responsive user experience across devices. Designing PWAs requires a deep understanding of web technologies and user interactions with both web and mobile interfaces.

Gesture-based interfaces are another example of innovation in UI/UX design. Gesture-based interfaces, such as those used in touchscreens and motion-sensing devices, provide an intuitive and natural way for users to interact with devices. Designing gesture-based interfaces requires a deep understanding of user interactions with touch and motion.

The use of biometrics in UI/UX design is also an example of innovation. Biometrics, such as fingerprint scanning and facial recognition, provide a secure and convenient way for users to authenticate and access devices and services. Designing for biometrics requires a deep understanding of user interactions with biometric sensors and security considerations.

In conclusion, innovative UI/UX solutions involve the use of new technologies, design trends, and user-centered approaches to create unique and engaging user experiences. By pushing the boundaries of traditional design and exploring new possibilities, designers can create innovative solutions that meet the evolving needs and preferences of users.

Industry-Specific UI/UX Case Studies

Industry-specific UI/UX case studies provide valuable insights into the unique challenges and opportunities faced by different industries in creating effective user experiences. These case studies highlight the importance of understanding industry-specific user needs and designing solutions that address those needs.

One example of an industry-specific UI/UX case study is the healthcare industry. In healthcare, UI/UX design plays a crucial role in creating user-friendly and accessible interfaces for patients, doctors, and healthcare providers. A notable example is the redesign of the Mayo Clinic's website. The redesign focused on improving usability, accessibility, and patient engagement by conducting user research and testing. The result was a more intuitive and accessible website that enhanced the overall patient experience.

Another example is the e-commerce industry. In e-commerce, UI/UX design is essential for creating seamless and engaging shopping experiences. A notable case study is the redesign of Amazon's mobile app. The redesign aimed to improve the user experience by enhancing navigation, search functionality, and personalization. By conducting user research and iterative testing, Amazon created a more intuitive and engaging mobile shopping experience that increased user satisfaction and sales.

The financial services industry also provides valuable UI/UX case studies. In financial services, UI/UX design is crucial for creating secure and user-friendly interfaces for banking, investing, and financial management. A notable example is the redesign of the Mint app. The redesign focused on improving usability, security, and user engagement by conducting user research and testing. The result was a more intuitive and secure financial management app that enhanced the overall user experience.

In the education industry, UI/UX design plays a crucial role in creating engaging and effective learning experiences. A notable case study is the redesign of the Khan Academy website. The redesign aimed to improve usability, accessibility, and student engagement by conducting user research and testing. By creating a more intuitive and accessible website, Khan Academy enhanced the overall learning experience for students.

The travel industry also provides valuable UI/UX case studies. In travel, UI/UX design is essential for creating seamless and engaging booking and travel experiences. A notable example is the redesign of the Airbnb app. The redesign focused on improving usability, search functionality, and personalization by conducting user research and iterative testing.

The result was a more intuitive and engaging travel booking experience that increased user satisfaction and bookings.

In the entertainment industry, UI/UX design plays a crucial role in creating engaging and immersive experiences for users. A notable case study is the redesign of Netflix's interface. The redesign aimed to improve usability, navigation, and personalization by conducting user research and testing. By creating a more intuitive and personalized interface, Netflix enhanced the overall user experience and increased user engagement and retention.

The automotive industry also provides valuable UI/UX case studies. In automotive, UI/UX design is crucial for creating user-friendly and engaging interfaces for in-car systems and digital services. A notable example is the redesign of Tesla's in-car interface. The redesign focused on improving usability, accessibility, and user engagement by conducting user research and testing. The result was a more intuitive and user-friendly in-car interface that enhanced the overall driving experience.

In the gaming industry, UI/UX design plays a crucial role in creating immersive and engaging gaming experiences. A notable case study is the redesign of the PlayStation interface. The redesign aimed to improve usability, navigation, and personalization by conducting user research and testing. By creating a more intuitive and personalized interface, PlayStation enhanced the overall gaming experience and increased user engagement.

The hospitality industry also provides valuable UI/UX case studies. In hospitality, UI/UX design is essential for creating seamless and engaging booking and guest experiences. A notable example is the redesign of the Marriott app. The redesign focused on improving usability, search functionality, and personalization by conducting user research and iterative testing. The result was a more intuitive and engaging travel booking experience that increased user satisfaction and bookings.

In conclusion, industry-specific UI/UX case studies provide valuable insights into the unique challenges and opportunities faced by different industries in creating effective user experiences. By understanding industry-specific user needs and designing solutions that address those needs, designers can create products that meet the unique requirements of each industry.

Chapter 17: The Future of UI/UX Design

Emerging Trends in UI/UX

Emerging trends in UI/UX design are driven by advancements in technology, changing user expectations, and new methodologies. These trends aim to create more intuitive, engaging, and inclusive user experiences.

One significant trend is the integration of artificial intelligence (AI) and machine learning in UI/UX design. AI can personalize user experiences by analyzing behavior patterns and preferences, making interfaces more adaptive and user-centric. For instance, AI can dynamically adjust the layout and content of a website to suit individual user needs, enhancing usability and engagement.

Voice user interfaces (VUIs) are gaining traction as voice-activated assistants like Siri, Alexa, and Google Assistant become more prevalent. Designing for VUIs involves creating intuitive voice commands and responses, which requires understanding natural language processing and user expectations for conversational interactions.

Augmented reality (AR) and virtual reality (VR) are transforming the way users interact with digital content. AR overlays digital information on the physical world, enhancing real-world experiences, while VR immerses users in entirely virtual environments. UI/UX designers must consider spatial design principles, 3D interactions, and sensory feedback to create effective AR and VR experiences.

Another trend is the focus on microinteractions, which are subtle, often unnoticed interactions that enhance user experience. These include animations, haptic feedback, and sound effects that provide immediate feedback and make the interface feel more responsive and engaging.

Dark mode design has become increasingly popular, offering a visually appealing and eye-strain-reducing alternative to traditional light mode. Designing for dark mode involves careful consideration of color palettes, contrast, and readability to ensure a consistent and accessible user experience.

Sustainability in UI/UX design is also emerging as a critical trend. Designers are considering the environmental impact of digital products and striving to create energy-efficient, eco-friendly designs. This includes optimizing code, reducing the need for excessive hardware resources, and promoting digital minimalism.

Inclusive design is gaining importance, with a focus on accessibility and creating products that cater to diverse user needs. This involves designing for users with disabilities, considering cultural differences, and ensuring that digital products are usable by people of all ages and backgrounds.

Neumorphism, a design trend that combines skeuomorphism and flat design, is making a comeback. It uses soft shadows and highlights to create a tactile, almost 3D effect on flat interfaces. While visually appealing, designers must balance aesthetics with usability to avoid potential accessibility issues.

The rise of no-code and low-code platforms is democratizing UI/UX design, allowing non-technical users to create functional and aesthetically pleasing digital products. These platforms use visual interfaces and pre-built components, enabling rapid prototyping and reducing the time to market.

Lastly, data-driven design is becoming more prevalent. By leveraging user data and analytics, designers can make informed decisions, optimize user flows, and continuously improve the user experience. Tools like heatmaps, A/B testing, and user feedback are essential for understanding user behavior and preferences.

In conclusion, the future of UI/UX design is shaped by technological advancements, evolving user needs, and a growing emphasis on inclusivity and sustainability. By staying abreast of these trends, designers can create innovative, user-centric, and impactful digital experiences.

The Impact of New Technologies

The rapid advancement of new technologies is profoundly impacting the field of UI/UX design. These technologies are not only changing the way designers create interfaces but also how users interact with digital products.

One of the most significant impacts is from artificial intelligence (AI) and machine learning. AI can analyze vast amounts of user data to identify patterns and preferences, allowing for highly personalized user experiences. For example, recommendation systems on e-commerce sites use AI to suggest products based on previous purchases and browsing behavior, enhancing user satisfaction and engagement.

Blockchain technology is also influencing UI/UX design, particularly in applications requiring high security and transparency. Blockchain's decentralized nature ensures that data is secure and immutable, which is crucial for financial, healthcare, and identity verification applications. Designers must consider how to present complex blockchain transactions in a user-friendly manner.

The Internet of Things (IoT) is creating new interaction paradigms as everyday objects become connected. Designers must consider how users will interact with smart devices through various interfaces, such as mobile apps, voice commands, and automated systems. This requires a deep understanding of context-aware design and seamless user experiences across different devices.

5G technology is set to revolutionize UI/UX design by providing ultra-fast internet speeds and low latency. This will enable more immersive experiences, such as high-definition video streaming, real-time gaming, and advanced AR/VR applications. Designers will need to leverage these capabilities to create richer, more interactive digital experiences.

Biometric authentication, including fingerprint scanning, facial recognition, and voice recognition, is becoming more common. This technology enhances security and convenience, but designers must ensure that these methods are intuitive and privacy-compliant. For example, facial recognition should work in various lighting conditions and accommodate different facial features.

Wearable technology, such as smartwatches and fitness trackers, is influencing UI/UX design by introducing new ways for users to interact with digital content. These devices often have small screens and limited input methods, requiring minimalist and efficient interface designs. Designers must prioritize essential information and interactions to provide a seamless user experience on wearables.

Quantum computing, though still in its infancy, promises to revolutionize problem-solving capabilities and data processing speeds. As quantum computing becomes more accessible, UI/UX designers will need to consider how to harness this power for complex simulations, predictive analytics, and other advanced applications.

Natural Language Processing (NLP) is improving the way users interact with systems through text and voice. Chatbots and virtual assistants powered by NLP can provide more accurate and context-aware responses, enhancing user satisfaction. Designers must create intuitive conversational interfaces that understand and respond to user queries effectively.

Edge computing is reducing latency by processing data closer to the source, rather than relying on centralized cloud servers. This is particularly beneficial for applications requiring real-time processing, such as autonomous vehicles and industrial IoT. UI/UX designers must consider how to provide immediate feedback and seamless interactions in edge computing environments.

Lastly, advancements in display technologies, such as foldable screens and e-ink displays, are offering new opportunities for innovative UI/UX designs. Foldable screens allow for dynamic interfaces that can change form factors, while e-ink displays provide energy-efficient options for devices like e-readers. Designers must adapt to these new form factors and create flexible, responsive interfaces.

In summary, new technologies are continually reshaping the landscape of UI/UX design. By understanding and leveraging these technologies, designers can create more engaging, secure, and efficient user experiences that meet the evolving needs of users.

The Role of UI/UX in the Metaverse

The metaverse represents a collective virtual shared space, created by the convergence of virtually enhanced physical reality and physically persistent virtual spaces. It encompasses augmented reality (AR), virtual reality (VR), and other immersive digital experiences. UI/UX design plays a critical role in shaping the user experience within this expansive digital ecosystem.

In the metaverse, the principles of UI/UX design must adapt to a three-dimensional, immersive environment. Traditional 2D interfaces give way to 3D spatial design, where users interact with objects and interfaces in a manner akin to the physical world. This shift necessitates a deep understanding of spatial relationships, depth perception, and intuitive interaction patterns.

Designing for the metaverse requires creating intuitive navigation systems that allow users to move seamlessly within virtual spaces. This involves understanding how users perceive and interact with the virtual environment, and designing controls that feel natural and responsive. For example, teleportation, flying, and walking are common navigation methods in VR environments, each requiring a unique design approach.

Avatar customization is a significant aspect of the metaverse experience. Users should have the ability to create and personalize their digital personas, reflecting their identity and preferences. UI/UX designers must ensure that the customization process is user-friendly and offers a wide range of options to cater to diverse user needs.

Social interactions in the metaverse are another critical area of focus. Designing virtual spaces where users can communicate, collaborate, and socialize effectively is paramount. This involves creating intuitive interfaces for voice and text communication, as well as designing virtual environments that facilitate social engagement and community building.

The metaverse also introduces new opportunities for immersive storytelling and experiential design. Brands and creators can craft unique, interactive experiences that engage users in novel ways. UI/UX designers must consider how to guide users through these experiences, balancing narrative flow with interactivity to create compelling and memorable journeys.

Accessibility in the metaverse is crucial to ensure that virtual experiences are inclusive. Designers must consider various accessibility needs, such as providing alternative navigation methods for users with mobility impairments, designing visual elements with sufficient contrast for users with visual impairments, and offering customizable interaction modes.

Privacy and security are paramount in the metaverse. Users will be sharing personal data and engaging in transactions within virtual spaces, necessitating robust security measures. UI/UX designers must create transparent interfaces that clearly communicate privacy policies and provide users with control over their data.

Cross-platform compatibility is essential in the metaverse, as users will access virtual environments from various devices, including VR headsets, AR glasses, smartphones, and computers. Designers must ensure a consistent and seamless experience across different platforms, considering the unique interaction patterns and capabilities of each device.

Monetization strategies in the metaverse, such as virtual goods, real estate, and experiences, require careful UI/UX design. Virtual marketplaces must offer an intuitive and secure shopping experience, with clear information about products and services. Designers must also consider the integration of digital currencies and blockchain technology for secure transactions.

Lastly, the ethical considerations of designing for the metaverse cannot be overlooked. UI/UX designers must ensure that virtual experiences are created with empathy and respect for users, avoiding manipulative design practices and prioritizing user well-being. This includes addressing issues like digital addiction, cyberbullying, and the psychological impact of immersive environments.

In conclusion, the role of UI/UX design in the metaverse is multifaceted and pivotal. By embracing the unique challenges and opportunities of this emerging digital frontier, designers can create immersive, engaging, and inclusive virtual experiences that redefine the way users interact with digital content.

Ethical Considerations for Future Designs

As UI/UX design continues to evolve, ethical considerations are becoming increasingly important. Designers have a responsibility to create experiences that are not only functional and engaging but also ethical and respectful of users' rights and well-being.

One major ethical consideration is user privacy. With the increasing amount of data collected by digital products, designers must ensure that user data is handled responsibly. This involves implementing transparent data collection practices, allowing users to control their data, and ensuring that data is securely stored and processed. Designers should prioritize privacy by design, embedding privacy features into the product development process from the outset.

Inclusivity and accessibility are critical ethical aspects of UI/UX design. Designers must strive to create experiences that are usable by people of all abilities and backgrounds. This includes designing for users with disabilities, considering cultural and linguistic diversity, and ensuring that products are accessible to all age groups. By adopting inclusive design principles, designers can create products that are equitable and empowering.

Another ethical consideration is avoiding dark patterns, which are design practices that manipulate users into taking actions they might not otherwise choose. Examples include hidden costs, tricky opt-out mechanisms, and deliberately confusing interfaces. Ethical design prioritizes user autonomy and informed consent, ensuring that users can make decisions that align with their best interests.

Designing for user well-being is also essential. This involves creating products that promote healthy usage patterns and do not contribute to digital addiction or negative mental health outcomes. Features like usage reminders, screen time tracking, and promoting breaks can help users maintain a balanced relationship with technology.

The ethical implications of persuasive design and gamification must be carefully considered. While these techniques can enhance user engagement, they should not be used to exploit users or encourage harmful behaviors. Designers must balance motivation and manipulation, ensuring that persuasive elements are used ethically and transparently.

Sustainability is another important ethical consideration in UI/UX design. Digital products have an environmental impact, from energy consumption to electronic waste. Designers can contribute to sustainability by creating energy-efficient products, promoting digital minimalism, and considering the lifecycle of digital devices. This involves designing for longevity and encouraging responsible disposal and recycling of electronic components.

Transparency in design is crucial for building trust with users. This includes clearly communicating the purpose of data collection, explaining how algorithms make decisions, and providing users with insight into how their data is used. Transparent design fosters trust and allows users to make informed choices about their interactions with digital products.

The rise of AI and machine learning in UI/UX design brings additional ethical considerations. AI systems can perpetuate biases present in the data they are trained on, leading to discriminatory outcomes. Designers must ensure that AI-driven features are fair and unbiased, conducting thorough testing and validation to identify and mitigate any potential biases.

Ethical considerations also extend to the impact of design on society. Designers should be aware of the broader societal implications of their work, considering how digital products influence social interactions, political discourse, and cultural norms. This involves reflecting on the potential consequences of design decisions and striving to create products that have a positive social impact.

In conclusion, ethical considerations are integral to the future of UI/UX design. By prioritizing privacy, inclusivity, transparency, and sustainability, designers can create digital experiences that are not only effective and engaging but also ethical and respectful of users' rights and well-being. Embracing ethical design principles ensures that UI/UX design contributes positively to individuals and society as a whole.

Preparing for Future Challenges

The field of UI/UX design is continuously evolving, presenting new challenges that designers must prepare for to stay relevant and effective. Anticipating and adapting to these challenges is crucial for creating innovative and user-centric digital experiences.

One of the primary challenges is keeping up with rapid technological advancements. As new technologies emerge, designers must quickly learn and integrate these tools into their workflows. This requires continuous learning and staying informed about the latest trends, tools, and best practices. Designers should actively participate in professional development opportunities, such as workshops, courses, and conferences, to keep their skills current.

The increasing complexity of digital ecosystems presents another challenge. Designers must consider how their products interact with a wide range of devices, platforms, and services. This involves designing for cross-platform compatibility, ensuring a seamless user experience across different contexts, and addressing the unique constraints and opportunities of each platform.

User expectations are continually evolving, driven by advancements in technology and changes in societal norms. Designers must stay attuned to these shifts, conducting regular user research to understand emerging needs and preferences. This involves using both qualitative and quantitative research methods to gather insights and iterating on designs based on user feedback.

The growing importance of data privacy and security poses significant challenges for UI/UX designers. Designers must create interfaces that are secure by design, ensuring that user data is protected from breaches and misuse. This involves implementing robust security measures, such as encryption and secure authentication, and designing transparent privacy controls that allow users to manage their data effectively.

Inclusivity and accessibility will continue to be crucial challenges. Designers must strive to create products that are usable by people of all abilities and backgrounds. This involves adopting inclusive design practices, such as designing for screen readers, providing alternative text for images, and ensuring that interfaces are navigable using assistive technologies. Regular accessibility audits and user testing with diverse populations can help identify and address potential barriers.

The rise of remote work and global collaboration introduces challenges related to communication and collaboration within design teams. Designers must leverage collaborative tools and platforms to facilitate seamless teamwork, regardless of physical location. This involves adopting agile methodologies, using version control systems, and maintaining clear and open lines of communication to ensure that team members are aligned and productive.

The increasing use of AI and automation in design processes presents both opportunities and challenges. While AI can enhance efficiency and personalization, designers must ensure that AI-driven features are ethical, unbiased, and transparent. This involves understanding the limitations of AI, conducting thorough testing, and being mindful of the ethical implications of automated decisions.

The need for sustainability in design is becoming more urgent as environmental concerns grow. Designers must consider the environmental impact of their products and strive to create energy-efficient, sustainable designs. This involves optimizing performance, reducing unnecessary features, and promoting digital minimalism. Additionally, designers should advocate for sustainable practices within their organizations and educate users about the environmental impact of their digital behaviors.

Lastly, preparing for future challenges involves fostering a culture of innovation and experimentation. Designers should be encouraged to explore new ideas, take risks, and learn from failures. This involves creating an environment where experimentation is valued, and iterative design processes are embraced. By fostering a culture of continuous improvement and innovation, design teams can stay ahead of emerging challenges and create groundbreaking digital experiences.

In summary, preparing for future challenges in UI/UX design requires continuous learning, staying attuned to user needs, ensuring inclusivity and accessibility, addressing privacy and security concerns, leveraging collaborative tools, and fostering a culture of innovation. By anticipating and adapting to these challenges, designers can create innovative, user-centric digital experiences that meet the evolving needs of users and the industry.

Chapter 18: Building a Career in UI/UX Design

Skills and Qualifications Needed

Building a successful career in UI/UX design requires a combination of technical skills, creative abilities, and soft skills. These qualifications enable designers to create compelling user experiences and collaborate effectively with multidisciplinary teams.

Firstly, a strong foundation in design principles is essential. This includes understanding color theory, typography, layout, and visual hierarchy. These principles help designers create aesthetically pleasing and functional interfaces. Formal education in design, such as a degree in graphic design, interaction design, or a related field, can provide a solid foundation.

Proficiency in design tools is crucial for creating and prototyping UI/UX designs. Common tools include Adobe Creative Suite (Photoshop, Illustrator), Sketch, Figma, and Adobe XD. These tools allow designers to create wireframes, mockups, and interactive prototypes, facilitating the design process and enabling effective communication with stakeholders.

Knowledge of front-end development is increasingly valuable for UI/UX designers. Understanding HTML, CSS, and JavaScript helps designers create realistic prototypes and collaborate more effectively with developers. While not all designers need to code, having a basic understanding of these technologies can enhance design feasibility and implementation.

User research skills are vital for creating user-centric designs. This involves conducting user interviews, surveys, and usability testing to gather insights into user needs and behaviors. Analyzing this data helps designers make informed decisions and create interfaces that meet user expectations. Courses or certifications in user research methods can be beneficial.

Critical thinking and problem-solving abilities are essential for addressing design challenges. UI/UX designers must be able to identify problems, generate creative solutions, and iterate on designs based on user feedback. This requires a balance of analytical and creative thinking, as well as the ability to adapt to changing requirements.

Strong communication skills are necessary for collaborating with team members and presenting design ideas to stakeholders. Designers must be able to articulate their design rationale, provide constructive feedback, and incorporate feedback from others. This involves both verbal and written communication, as well as the ability to create clear and compelling presentations.

Empathy is a key trait for UI/UX designers, as it allows them to understand and prioritize user needs. Designers must put themselves in the users' shoes, considering their emotions, motivations, and pain points. This user-centric mindset helps create interfaces that are intuitive, accessible, and satisfying.

Attention to detail is crucial for creating polished and professional designs. This involves meticulous consideration of every element, from typography and spacing to interactions and animations. A keen eye for detail ensures that the final product is cohesive and meets high quality standards.

Adaptability and a willingness to learn are important qualities for staying current in the fast evolving field of UI/UX design. Designers must keep up with new trends, tools, and methodologies, continuously expanding their skill set. This involves pursuing ongoing education through workshops, online courses, and industry conferences.

Portfolio development is a critical aspect of building a career in UI/UX design. A strong portfolio showcases a designer's skills, process, and range of work. It should include case studies that highlight problem-solving abilities, user research, and the impact of design decisions. Regularly updating the portfolio with new projects and refining its presentation is essential.

Networking and professional development can significantly enhance career opportunities. Joining design communities, attending industry events, and connecting with other professionals can provide valuable insights, mentorship, and job leads. Active participation in the design community helps build a reputation and opens doors to new opportunities.

In conclusion, building a career in UI/UX design requires a diverse set of skills and qualifications. By developing technical expertise, creative abilities, and soft skills, designers can create impactful user experiences and advance in their careers. Continuous learning, portfolio development, and networking are essential for staying competitive in this dynamic field.

Creating a UI/UX Portfolio

Creating a compelling UI/UX portfolio is crucial for showcasing your skills, experience, and design thinking process. A well-crafted portfolio demonstrates your ability to solve real-world problems and highlights your best work to potential employers or clients.

Begin by selecting a portfolio platform that suits your needs. Popular options include personal websites, Behance, Dribbble, and portfolio-specific platforms like Cargo or Adobe Portfolio. Choose a platform that allows you to showcase your work effectively and offers flexibility in presentation.

Start with an engaging introduction or about me section. This should include a brief overview of your background, design philosophy, and areas of expertise. Highlight what makes you unique as a designer and provide context about your career journey.

Your portfolio should feature a curated selection of projects that demonstrate your range and capabilities. Each project should include a detailed case study that outlines the design process, from initial research and ideation to final implementation and results. This helps potential employers understand your problem-solving approach and the impact of your work.

For each project, clearly define the problem or challenge you aimed to address. Explain the context, objectives, and constraints of the project. This sets the stage for showcasing how you approached the design process and the solutions you developed.

Include user research and insights to demonstrate your user-centered design approach. Describe the methods you used, such as user interviews, surveys, or usability testing, and present key findings that informed your design decisions. Highlight how you translated user needs into actionable design requirements.

Showcase your design process through sketches, wireframes, and prototypes. This visual documentation provides a glimpse into your iterative design approach and how you refined your ideas. Include annotations or brief explanations to guide viewers through your thought process.

Present the final design with high-quality visuals and interactive prototypes. Highlight key features, interactions, and visual elements that make your design effective. Use mockups or real-world examples to show how your design works in context.

Discuss the results and impact of your design. This could include quantitative metrics, such as improved conversion rates or user satisfaction scores, or qualitative feedback from users or stakeholders. Demonstrating the effectiveness of your design solutions reinforces your ability to deliver value.

Keep your portfolio organized and easy to navigate. Use a clean, consistent layout and categorize projects by type or industry if applicable. Ensure that your portfolio is accessible on different devices, including desktops, tablets, and smartphones.

In addition to project case studies, consider including a section for additional skills or services you offer. This could include UI/UX audits, user research, or design consultations. Highlighting these services can attract clients or employers looking for specific expertise.

Regularly update your portfolio with new projects and refine existing case studies. This shows that you are active in your field and continuously improving your skills. Remove outdated or less relevant work to keep your portfolio focused and impactful.

Networking and sharing your portfolio within the design community can also enhance your visibility. Participate in design forums, social media platforms, and industry events to showcase your work and connect with other professionals. Building a network of peers and mentors can lead to new opportunities and collaborations.

In conclusion, creating a UI/UX portfolio requires careful selection of projects, clear presentation of your design process, and regular updates to showcase your growth as a designer. By effectively communicating your skills and experience, you can attract potential employers or clients and advance your career in UI/UX design.

Networking and Professional Development

Networking and professional development are essential components of building a successful career in UI/UX design. Engaging with the design community, attending events, and continuously improving your skills can open doors to new opportunities and enhance your professional growth.

Start by joining design communities and online forums where you can connect with other UI/UX professionals. Platforms like LinkedIn, Twitter, and specialized design forums such as Designer Hangout or UX Mastery provide opportunities to share knowledge, ask questions, and engage in discussions. Active participation in these communities can help you stay informed about industry trends and best practices.

Attending industry conferences, workshops, and meetups is another effective way to network and develop professionally. Events like UX Week, Interaction, and local UX meetups offer opportunities to learn from industry leaders, participate in hands-on workshops, and connect with peers. These events can provide valuable insights, inspiration, and potential job leads.

Consider joining professional organizations such as the Interaction Design Association (IxDA), User Experience Professionals Association (UXPA), or local design groups. Membership in these organizations often provides access to resources, events, and a network of professionals that can support your career growth.

Mentorship is a powerful tool for professional development. Seek out experienced designers who can provide guidance, feedback, and support as you navigate your career. Mentors can offer valuable insights into the industry, help you refine your skills, and provide advice on career advancement. Conversely, consider mentoring junior designers to give back to the community and further develop your leadership skills.

Continuing education is crucial for staying current in the rapidly evolving field of UI/UX design. Pursue additional certifications, courses, and workshops to expand your knowledge and skills. Platforms like Coursera, Udemy, and LinkedIn Learning offer a wide range of courses on topics such as user research, interaction design, and design thinking. Staying updated with the latest tools and methodologies will enhance your expertise and competitiveness.

Writing and speaking about UI/UX design can also contribute to your professional development. Consider starting a blog, contributing to industry publications, or speaking at conferences and meetups. Sharing your knowledge and experiences not only establishes you as a thought leader but also helps you articulate your ideas and gain feedback from the community.

Collaborating on open-source projects or volunteering for non-profit organizations can provide valuable hands-on experience and expand your network. These opportunities allow you to work on diverse projects, develop new skills, and demonstrate your commitment to the field. Additionally, they can lead to connections with like-minded professionals and potential job opportunities.

Building a strong online presence is important for networking and professional development. Maintain an up-to-date LinkedIn profile, showcase your portfolio on platforms like Behance or Dribbble, and engage with the design community on social media. A well-crafted online presence can attract potential employers, clients, and collaborators.

Participating in design competitions and hackathons is another way to challenge yourself, showcase your skills, and network with other professionals. These events provide opportunities to work on innovative projects, receive feedback from judges and peers, and gain recognition in the industry.

In conclusion, networking and professional development are vital for advancing your career in UI/UX design. By actively engaging with the design community, seeking mentorship, continuing your education, and sharing your knowledge, you can build a strong professional network and enhance your skills. These efforts will open doors to new opportunities and support your long-term career growth.

Job Search and Interview Tips

The job search process in UI/UX design can be competitive, but with the right strategies and preparation, you can increase your chances of landing your desired role. Here are some tips to help you navigate the job search and interview process effectively.

Begin by clearly defining your career goals and identifying the type of UI/UX roles you are interested in. Whether you aim to work in a startup, a large corporation, or as a freelancer, having a clear vision will guide your job search and help you target relevant opportunities.

Tailor your resume and portfolio for each job application. Highlight the skills and experiences that are most relevant to the specific role and company. Use keywords from the job description to align your application with the employer's requirements. A customized application demonstrates your genuine interest in the position and increases your chances of getting noticed.

Leverage your network to find job opportunities. Reach out to connections in the industry, attend networking events, and engage with online design communities. Referrals from people within your network can significantly improve your chances of securing an interview.

When applying for jobs, write a compelling cover letter that complements your resume and portfolio. Use the cover letter to explain why you are interested in the role, how your skills and experiences make you a good fit, and what you can contribute to the company. Personalize each cover letter to show your understanding of the company and its needs.

Prepare thoroughly for interviews by researching the company, its products, and its design philosophy. Understand the company's target audience, market position, and recent projects. This knowledge will help you answer questions more effectively and demonstrate your enthusiasm for the role.

Practice common UI/UX interview questions and prepare your answers. Questions may cover topics such as your design process, user research methods, problem-solving approaches, and specific projects from your portfolio. Be ready to discuss your design decisions, the challenges you faced, and the outcomes of your projects.

Prepare a set of questions to ask the interviewer. This shows your interest in the role and helps you assess if the company is the right fit for you. Questions can include inquiries about the design team structure, the company's design process, opportunities for professional development, and the tools and technologies used.

During the interview, be clear and concise in your responses. Use examples from your portfolio to illustrate your points and provide context. If you don't know the answer to a question, it's okay to admit it and explain how you would approach finding a solution. Demonstrating a problem-solving mindset is often more valuable than having all the answers.

Showcase your communication and collaboration skills. UI/UX design often involves working closely with cross-functional teams, so employers look for candidates who can communicate effectively and work well with others. Highlight experiences where you successfully collaborated with developers, product managers, or other stakeholders.

Follow up after the interview with a thank-you email. Express your appreciation for the opportunity to interview and reiterate your interest in the role. A thoughtful follow-up can leave a positive impression and keep you top of mind with the hiring team.

In conclusion, a successful job search in UI/UX design involves a combination of targeted applications, thorough preparation, and effective networking. By tailoring your resume and portfolio, practicing interview questions, and showcasing your skills and enthusiasm, you can increase your chances of landing your desired role. Continuous learning and engagement with the design community will further support your career growth.

Continuous Learning and Growth

Continuous learning and growth are essential for maintaining a successful and fulfilling career in UI/UX design. The field is constantly evolving, and staying updated with the latest trends, tools, and methodologies is crucial for staying competitive and delivering high-quality designs.

One of the most effective ways to ensure continuous learning is to regularly take courses and attend workshops. Online platforms like Coursera, Udemy, and LinkedIn Learning offer a wide range of courses on various aspects of UI/UX design, from user research and interaction design to advanced prototyping techniques. Enrolling in these courses allows you to deepen your knowledge and acquire new skills at your own pace.

Participating in design bootcamps can also provide intensive, hands-on learning experiences. Bootcamps like General Assembly and Designlab offer immersive programs that cover essential design skills and provide opportunities to work on real-world projects. These programs often include mentorship and feedback from industry professionals, which can significantly enhance your learning process.

Reading books and articles on UI/UX design is another valuable way to stay informed and inspired. Books such as "Don't Make Me Think" by Steve Krug, "The Design of Everyday Things" by Don Norman, and "Hooked" by Nir Eyal offer foundational knowledge and insights into user behavior and design principles. Following design blogs, subscribing to newsletters, and reading articles from sources like Smashing Magazine, A List Apart, and UX Collective can keep you updated with the latest industry trends and best practices.

Engaging with the design community through forums, social media, and professional organizations can provide opportunities for knowledge sharing and networking. Platforms like Designer Hangout, UX Mastery, and Reddit's r/userexperience offer spaces for discussions, advice, and collaboration. Connecting with other designers can help you gain different perspectives, receive feedback on your work, and stay motivated.

Attending industry conferences and events is another excellent way to learn from experts and network with peers. Conferences like UX Week, Interaction, and local UX meetups feature talks, workshops, and panels on various design topics. These events provide opportunities to learn about cutting-edge research, innovative techniques, and emerging trends in UI/UX design.

Practicing design challenges and side projects can help you apply new skills and experiment with different design approaches. Participating in design challenges on platforms like Dribbble or engaging in personal projects allows you to explore creative ideas, build your portfolio, and refine your design process. These activities also demonstrate your passion and commitment to continuous improvement.

Seeking feedback on your work is crucial for growth. Share your designs with colleagues, mentors, or online design communities to receive constructive feedback. Critiques can help you identify areas for improvement, validate your design decisions, and gain new insights. Embracing feedback as a tool for learning rather than criticism can accelerate your growth as a designer.

Staying curious and open to new experiences is essential for continuous learning. Explore related fields such as psychology, anthropology, or marketing to gain a broader understanding of human behavior and user needs. This interdisciplinary knowledge can enhance your ability to create user-centered designs and solve complex problems.

In conclusion, continuous learning and growth in UI/UX design require a proactive and multifaceted approach. By taking courses, reading books and articles, engaging with the design community, attending events, practicing design challenges, and seeking feedback, you can stay updated and improve your skills. Embracing a mindset of lifelong learning will ensure that you remain adaptable and successful in the dynamic field of UI/UX design.

Chapter 19: Tools and Resources for UI/UX Designers

Design Software and Tools

To excel in UI/UX design, familiarity with various design software and tools is essential. These tools help designers create, prototype, and test their designs efficiently.

Figma is a popular design tool known for its collaboration features. It allows multiple designers to work on the same project in real-time, making it ideal for team projects. Its intuitive interface and powerful prototyping capabilities make it a favorite among designers.

Sketch is another widely used tool, particularly among Mac users. It offers a range of plugins and integrations that enhance its functionality, making it suitable for both UI and UX design tasks.

Adobe XD is part of the Adobe Creative Cloud suite and integrates well with other Adobe products like Photoshop and Illustrator. It offers robust prototyping features and supports voice interactions, which is useful for designing voice-based user interfaces.

InVision is primarily known for its prototyping and collaboration features. It allows designers to create interactive prototypes and gather feedback from stakeholders, streamlining the design process.

Axure RP is a powerful tool for creating detailed wireframes and prototypes. It is often used for complex projects that require advanced interactions and dynamic content.

Balsamiq is a user-friendly wireframing tool that focuses on low-fidelity designs. It is ideal for quickly sketching out ideas and getting early feedback.

Principle is a tool for creating animated and interactive user interfaces. It is particularly useful for designing microinteractions and motion graphics.

Framer is a design tool that combines visual design with code. It allows designers to create high-fidelity prototypes that can be tested and refined with real user interactions.

Marvel is another tool that supports design, prototyping, and collaboration. It offers features like user testing and handoff to developers, making it a comprehensive tool for the entire design process.

Zeplin is a collaboration tool that bridges the gap between designers and developers. It generates style guides and assets that developers can use to implement the design accurately.

Online Courses and Tutorials

Learning UI/UX design is an ongoing process, and online courses and tutorials are valuable resources for designers at all levels.

Coursera offers courses from top universities and institutions. For example, the "UI/UX Design Specialization" by the California Institute of the Arts covers the fundamentals of UI/UX design, including wireframing, prototyping, and user research.

Udemy provides a vast array of UI/UX design courses. "User Experience Design Essentials - Adobe XD UI UX Design" is a popular course that teaches the basics of UI/UX design using Adobe XD.

Interaction Design Foundation (IDF) is a platform dedicated to design education. It offers comprehensive courses on various aspects of UI/UX design, taught by industry experts.

LinkedIn Learning (formerly Lynda.com) provides courses on UI/UX design, covering both basic and advanced topics. Courses like "UX Design: From Concept to Prototype" offer practical insights into the design process.

Skillshare is another platform with a range of UI/UX design courses. "Intro to UX: Fundamentals of Usability" is a beginner-friendly course that covers the essentials of usability and user experience design.

Google offers a "UX Design Professional Certificate" through Coursera. This program is designed to equip learners with job-ready skills in UX design, covering topics like user research, wireframing, and prototyping.

YouTube is a valuable resource for free tutorials on UI/UX design. Channels like "The Futur" and "DesignCourse" provide high-quality content on various design topics.

Nielsen Norman Group offers specialized courses and tutorials on UX design. Their content is research-based and focuses on practical applications of UX principles.

Adobe's website offers tutorials and resources for using Adobe XD and other Adobe products in UI/UX design. These tutorials range from beginner to advanced levels.

Smashing Magazine provides articles, tutorials, and eBooks on UI/UX design. Their content is written by industry professionals and covers a wide range of design topics.

Books and Articles

Books and articles are excellent resources for deepening your understanding of UI/UX design principles and practices.

"Don't Make Me Think" by Steve Krug is a classic book on web usability. It emphasizes the importance of intuitive design and provides practical advice for creating user-friendly interfaces.

"The Design of Everyday Things" by Don Norman explores the psychology behind design and usability. It is a foundational text for understanding user-centered design principles.

"Hooked: How to Build Habit-Forming Products" by Nir Eyal delves into the psychology of user behavior and how to design products that engage and retain users.

"About Face: The Essentials of Interaction Design" by Alan Cooper is a comprehensive guide to interaction design. It covers everything from fundamental principles to advanced techniques.

"A Project Guide to UX Design" by Russ Unger and Carolyn Chandler provides a practical framework for managing UX design projects. It covers key aspects of the design process, from research to implementation.

"Lean UX" by Jeff Gothelf and Josh Seiden introduces a collaborative approach to UX design, emphasizing rapid experimentation and iteration.

"Designing for Emotion" by Aarron Walter explores how to create emotionally engaging user experiences. It provides insights into using humor, empathy, and personality in design.

"The Elements of User Experience" by Jesse James Garrett outlines a framework for understanding the different aspects of user experience design. It is a must-read for anyone new to the field.

"UX for Lean Startups" by Laura Klein offers practical advice for applying UX principles in a startup environment. It focuses on building products that meet user needs while minimizing waste.

Smashing Magazine publishes a variety of articles on UI/UX design. Their content is written by industry experts and covers a wide range of topics, from usability to visual design.

UI/UX Design Communities

Joining UI/UX design communities is a great way to connect with other designers, share knowledge, and stay updated on industry trends.

Dribbble is a popular platform for designers to showcase their work, get feedback, and discover inspiration. It also offers a job board for finding design-related opportunities.

Behance is another platform for designers to display their portfolios and connect with other creatives. It is part of the Adobe family and integrates well with Adobe Creative Cloud tools.

UX Design Community on LinkedIn is a group where professionals share articles, job postings, and discussions related to UI/UX design. It's a great place to network and learn from others in the field.

Designer Hangout is a Slack community for UX designers. It provides a space for designers to ask questions, share resources, and discuss industry trends.

Reddit has several UI/UX design-related subreddits, such as r/userexperience and r/web_design. These communities are great for asking questions, sharing projects, and discussing design topics.

Meetup is a platform for finding and organizing local events and meetups. Many cities have UI/UX design meetups where designers can network and learn from each other.

The Interaction Design Foundation (IDF) offers an online community where members can participate in discussions, attend webinars, and access exclusive content.

Smashing Magazine's forums provide a space for designers to discuss articles, ask for feedback, and share resources. It is a supportive community with a wealth of knowledge.

Medium is a platform where designers share articles and case studies on UI/UX design. Following publications like "UX Collective" and "Prototypr" can provide valuable insights and inspiration.

Slack channels like "Designer Hangout" and "UX Mastery" offer real-time discussions on various UI/UX topics. These communities are excellent for getting quick feedback and advice.

Conferences and Events

Attending UI/UX design conferences and events is an excellent way to learn from industry leaders, network with peers, and stay updated on the latest trends and technologies.

UXPA International is one of the largest conferences for UX professionals. It covers a wide range of topics, from usability testing to interaction design, and attracts speakers from leading companies.

Interaction by IxDA is an annual conference organized by the Interaction Design Association. It features talks, workshops, and networking opportunities focused on interaction design.

Smashing Conference is organized by Smashing Magazine and offers events in various cities around the world. It covers topics like web design, UX, and front-end development.

Adobe MAX is Adobe's annual creative conference. It includes sessions on UI/UX design, showcasing the latest features in Adobe products and offering hands-on workshops.

An Event Apart is a conference series focused on web design and development. It covers topics like UX, accessibility, and responsive design, with sessions from industry experts.

NN/g UX Conference is organized by the Nielsen Norman Group and offers in-depth training on various UX topics. It is known for its practical, research-based approach.

Awwwards Conference brings together designers, developers, and digital creatives to discuss the future of web design. It includes talks, workshops, and networking events.

Designers + Geeks is a series of events held in various cities, featuring talks on design, technology, and entrepreneurship. It is a great opportunity to network with like-minded professionals.

UX Australia is the premier UX design conference in Australia. It offers presentations and workshops on a wide range of UX topics, from research to design strategy.

Web Summit is one of the largest technology conferences in the world. It includes a dedicated track for design and UX, with speakers from top tech companies and startups.

Chapter 20: Practical Applications of UI/UX Design

Implementing UI/UX in Startups

In the fast-paced environment of startups, implementing effective UI/UX design can be a key differentiator. Startups often operate with limited resources and tight deadlines, making efficient design processes crucial.

One of the first steps for a startup is to establish a clear understanding of the target audience. Conducting user research early in the development process helps identify user needs and pain points. Methods such as surveys, interviews, and usability testing provide valuable insights that inform design decisions.

Creating user personas is another important task. Personas are fictional characters that represent different user types. They help the design team keep the users' needs and goals in mind throughout the design process.

Startups should also prioritize creating a minimum viable product (MVP) with essential features. The MVP approach allows for quick release and feedback gathering, which can be used to iterate and improve the product.

Wireframing and prototyping are essential for visualizing ideas and testing functionality. Tools like Figma, Sketch, and Adobe XD facilitate rapid prototyping and collaboration among team members.

Usability testing should be conducted regularly to identify issues and gather user feedback. Testing can be done with low-fidelity prototypes initially and then with high-fidelity prototypes or actual product versions.

Startups should also focus on creating a consistent visual design and brand identity. This includes defining color schemes, typography, and imagery that align with the brand's message and appeal to the target audience.

Responsive design is crucial for startups aiming to reach users across various devices. Ensuring that the product provides a seamless experience on desktops, tablets, and smartphones enhances usability and user satisfaction.

Iterative design is key in a startup environment. Regularly updating the product based on user feedback and performance metrics helps in refining the user experience and meeting evolving user needs.

Collaboration between designers, developers, and other stakeholders is vital. Using tools like Slack, Jira, and Asana can streamline communication and project management.

Startups should also consider the scalability of their design solutions. As the product grows, the design should be able to accommodate new features and functionality without compromising user experience.

UI/UX for E-commerce

Effective UI/UX design is critical for e-commerce platforms, as it directly impacts user engagement, conversion rates, and customer satisfaction. A well-designed e-commerce site can significantly enhance the shopping experience and drive sales.

The first step in designing for e-commerce is understanding the customer journey. Mapping out the user's path from product discovery to purchase helps identify potential pain points and areas for improvement.

Product pages should be designed to provide clear and comprehensive information. High quality images, detailed descriptions, and customer reviews are essential elements that help users make informed purchasing decisions.

A streamlined and intuitive navigation system is crucial for e-commerce sites. Categories, filters, and search functionalities should be designed to help users find products quickly and easily.

The checkout process should be simplified to minimize friction. This includes reducing the number of steps, offering multiple payment options, and ensuring that users can easily review their orders before purchase.

Mobile optimization is essential for e-commerce platforms, as a significant portion of users shop on mobile devices. Responsive design ensures that the site provides a seamless experience across all devices.

Personalization can greatly enhance the user experience in e-commerce. Features like personalized product recommendations, targeted promotions, and saved shopping carts help engage users and encourage repeat visits.

Security is a major concern for online shoppers. E-commerce sites should clearly communicate their security measures, such as encryption and secure payment gateways, to build trust with users.

User feedback and reviews play a crucial role in e-commerce. Incorporating user-generated content, such as reviews and ratings, can help build credibility and influence purchasing decisions.

Usability testing is vital for e-commerce platforms. Regular testing helps identify issues and optimize the user experience based on actual user behavior and feedback.

Performance is another key factor. Ensuring fast load times and smooth interactions can significantly improve user satisfaction and reduce bounce rates.

Visual design should be consistent with the brand identity and appealing to the target audience. This includes using appropriate color schemes, typography, and imagery that align with the brand's message.

UI/UX in Healthcare

Designing for healthcare involves unique challenges and considerations. UI/UX design in healthcare must prioritize usability, accessibility, and compliance with regulatory standards to ensure that medical applications are effective and user-friendly.

Understanding the needs of different user groups is crucial in healthcare design. This includes patients, healthcare providers, and administrative staff, each with distinct requirements and goals.

User research methods such as interviews, surveys, and observational studies help gather insights into the needs and pain points of healthcare users. This information informs the design process and ensures that solutions are user-centered.

Accessibility is a critical consideration in healthcare design. Applications should be designed to accommodate users with varying abilities, including those with visual, auditory, and motor impairments.

Compliance with regulatory standards such as HIPAA (Health Insurance Portability and Accountability Act) is essential. Ensuring that patient data is handled securely and confidentially is a top priority.

Designing intuitive and easy-to-use interfaces helps reduce the cognitive load on users. This is particularly important in healthcare, where users may be under stress or have limited technical proficiency.

Clear and consistent navigation is vital in healthcare applications. Users should be able to find the information they need quickly and easily, whether it's patient records, appointment scheduling, or medication management.

Error prevention and recovery are important design principles in healthcare. Ensuring that users can easily correct mistakes and providing clear feedback can help prevent errors that could have serious consequences.

Telehealth applications have become increasingly important. Designing for remote consultations requires ensuring that video and audio quality are high and that interfaces are simple and reliable.

Usability testing with real users is essential to identify issues and improve the user experience. Testing should include a diverse range of users to ensure that the application meets the needs of all user groups.

Visual design should focus on clarity and readability. Using appropriate color schemes, typography, and iconography helps ensure that information is easily understandable.

UI/UX for Enterprise Applications

Enterprise applications often involve complex workflows and large amounts of data. Effective UI/UX design can help streamline these processes and improve productivity for enterprise users.

Understanding the specific needs and workflows of enterprise users is crucial. User research methods such as contextual inquiries and task analysis help gather insights into how users interact with the application.

Designing for scalability is important in enterprise applications. As the organization grows, the application should be able to accommodate increasing data and users without compromising performance.

Consistency is key in enterprise design. Using a consistent design language and interaction patterns helps users learn the system more quickly and reduces the risk of errors.

Data visualization is an important aspect of enterprise applications. Designing effective charts, graphs, and dashboards helps users make sense of complex data and make informed decisions.

Performance is a critical consideration in enterprise applications. Ensuring fast load times and smooth interactions can significantly improve user satisfaction and productivity.

Security and compliance are essential in enterprise design. Ensuring that the application meets regulatory standards and protects sensitive data is a top priority.

Collaboration features are often important in enterprise applications. Designing tools that facilitate communication and collaboration among users can enhance productivity and streamline workflows.

User onboarding is an important aspect of enterprise design. Providing clear instructions, tutorials, and help resources can help new users get up to speed quickly.

Responsive design ensures that the application provides a seamless experience across different devices, including desktops, tablets, and smartphones.

Usability testing is vital for enterprise applications. Regular testing with real users helps identify issues and optimize the user experience based on actual user behavior and feedback.

UI/UX in Educational Technology

Educational technology (EdTech) presents unique challenges and opportunities for UI/UX designers. Designing effective EdTech applications involves creating engaging and accessible learning experiences for students and educators.

Understanding the needs of different user groups, including students, teachers, and administrators, is crucial. User research methods such as interviews, surveys, and usability testing help gather insights into the needs and pain points of these users.

Engagement is a key factor in EdTech design. Creating interactive and engaging learning experiences helps keep students motivated and enhances the learning process.

Accessibility is an important consideration in EdTech design. Ensuring that applications are usable by students with varying abilities, including those with disabilities, is essential.

Gamification can be an effective strategy in EdTech. Incorporating game-like elements such as points, badges, and leaderboards can enhance engagement and motivation.

Responsive design is crucial for EdTech applications, as students and teachers may use a variety of devices. Ensuring that the application provides a seamless experience across desktops, tablets, and smartphones is important.

Collaboration features can enhance the learning experience. Designing tools that facilitate communication and collaboration among students and teachers can support group projects and discussions.

User feedback and analytics are important in EdTech design. Gathering feedback from students and teachers and analyzing usage data helps identify areas for improvement and optimize the user experience.

Clear and intuitive navigation is vital in EdTech applications. Students and teachers should be able to find the information and tools they need quickly and easily.

Visual design should focus on clarity and readability. Using appropriate color schemes, typography, and iconography helps ensure that information is easily understandable.

Usability testing with real users is essential to identify issues and improve the user experience. Testing should include a diverse range of users to ensure that the application meets the needs of all user groups.